Logistics and
The Saudi Vision 2030

The Top 10 Logistics
Innovations to Facilitate the Vision

Dr. Fadye Saud Al Fayad

ISBN: 978-603-02-6953-2 (sc)
ISBN: 978-1-4834-8882-0 (e)

Lulu Publishing Services rev. date: 8/7/2018

Contents

Foreword

Some mention must be given to the astute leadership of Crown Prince Mohammed. Even before being appointed Crown Prince, he managed to point Saudi Arabia towards a vision of the future that capitalized on the Kingdom's long history of innovation, learning and cultural leadership in the world. With the introduction of the Saudi Vision 2030 the Crown Prince managed to bring all of the competing economic and cultural perspectives in the country in-line with a single socio-economic plan. This type of unique visionary leadership is rarely seen in the world and having it revitalize the Kingdom's economy and regional heritage is refreshing indeed. As with any new and innovative plan like the Vision 2030, it is imperative that executable initiatives be developed to support such plans and this is the ultimate purpose of this book. Logistics and a well-managed supply chain are at the center of the global economy. Thus, an improved understanding of how the most current logistics trends can affect positive change in the Kingdom's economic centers is vital. It is with this spirit of growth and development for the Kingdom that this book is written as a means to offer even the slightest bit of assistance to the advancement of the Crown Prince's vision for the future of the Kingdom as summarized in the Vision 2030 ideals.

Preface

The top ten logistics trends currently affecting change within the logistics industry are, of course, somewhat subjective in character. Firstly, it should be mentioned that the field of logistics is an incredibly diverse one and thus any discussion of trends within the industry is not meant to imply that these are the only factors affecting the industry. Rather, the discussion of the top ten trends in the logistics industry is meant to identify those critical paths to success in enacting the Vision 2030 ideals and to do so in a way that capitalizes on the meaningful economic work that has already been accomplished. Secondly, the top ten trends in the logistics industry discussed in the manner in which they might be integrated into the Kingdom's economic cities is only intended to function as a guideline. Perhaps one of the most important factors within any contemporary industry involves the element of adaptiveness and flexibility and this applies to logistics as well as any other industry. In essence, it should be noted that these top ten trends have been identified by the author to be those top ten trends most relevant to the Kingdom and its Vision 2030 rather than universal top ten trends though there is a great deal of crossover in this regard to be sure.

Acknowledgments

Praise be to Allah for everything Allah has blessed us with. Special Thanks to my family for standing by me and supporting me throughout the completion of this book. Recognition of the Crown Prince Mohammed Bin Salman must also be made for it is his personal drive and vision of 2030 for the Kingdom that inspires all of us in our quest to support Saudi Arabia locally, regionally and internationally.

Introduction

Saudi Arabia is recognized internationally as being the cultural and economic epicenter of the Middle East. However, the prescient forethought of Crown Prince Mohammad bin Salman has led to the development of a visionary plan designed to guide the nation to the forefront of the global economic model. This visionary plan is referred to as the Saudi Vision 2030 and it is intended to ensure that the Kingdom retains its leadership role in the region as well as become an international focus for investment, manufacturing and financial remediation. The topic upon which this book focuses relates to involves the identification of the top 10 logistics innovations. These are the top 10 logistics related innovations that are currently being explored, developed or deployed throughout the world. The logistics field and industry is, in large part, the backbone of the global economy. Without the logistics and supply chain industry developing technologically in the way it has, globalization itself would have been if not impossible then at the least much less economically feasible for many competitors.

These top 10 logistics innovations are subsequently examined in the context of their application and influence on the Vision 2030 and how it can be better achieved through logistics competencies. The economic diversity that is one of the Vision's core objectives for the Kingdom is one that is entirely dependent upon the development of logistics best practices within the country. The use of best practices has been shown to be an effective way in which a firm in any industry and any market can achieve competitive parity without investing in an enormous amount of research and development from the ground up. Rather, benchmarking best practices encourages a competitive firm to benefit from the investment other firms have made in areas of interest to that firm. This book offers an in-depth analysis and discussion of these top 10 logistics innovations that are currently revolutionizing how international business is being done.

At the heart of the matter is the Kingdom's long-term economic stability based on the principle of economic diversification. True economic diversification involves much more than merely setting up new factories in multiple industries and calling it a day as it were. Rather, true diversification implies re-imagining a national economy and erecting the mechanisms to affect a host of supporting industries that facilitate entirely new businesses. Essentially, just building new manufacturing and production facilities in the Kingdom would accomplish little if the Kingdom had poorly managed transportation facilities to move both raw materials and finished products into and out of these facilities. Consequently, it is this this economic diversification that forms the nucleus of this text's underlying premise. Additionally, it is also the economic diversification of the Kingdom that is the primary target within the context of the Vision 2030 series of objectives.

These Vision 2030 series of objectives are intended to provide a high degree of economic prosperity for the Kingdom. They are summarized in the official doctrine relating to the text of Vision where it states that: "Free market prices shall, in the long term, stimulate productivity and competitiveness among utility companies and open the door to investment and diversification of the energy mix in the Kingdom."[1] In effect, the Kingdom expects to develop a much more diversified economy by the year 2030 and in a manner that does not compromise its existing wealth and international stature. Furthermore, the supply chain is seen as a discipline that is rapidly changing but which also expresses a pervasive impact of global competitiveness as well. The logistics and supply chain fields are supporting activities that enable virtually all businesses and enterprises to either thrive or, alternatively, to fail if poorly managed. The table below summarizes just how pervasive this influence of the logistics environment is with respect to international competitiveness in the commercial sector:

Table 1: Competitive Influences on Logistics

Competitive Influence of Logistics	Features	Effects
Emergent Dynamics of Market Competition	- Firms are no longer isolated and independent agencies - Market competition is now characterized by firm capabilities and competencies as opposed to purely brands that are supported by marketing & communications competencies - Commoditization is forcing efficiencies across all markets - Service-oriented activities now gain clients/customers versus product/item based activities - Demand is concentrated in key markets - Suppliers/Vendors are being reduced in number - Almost all product life-cycles are being reduced	- Value added systems must be put in place - Sustainable competitive advantage must be achieved through more efficient core competencies and procedures versus the competition - Brand loyalty is increasingly less relevant and purchase decisions increasingly made at point of purchase - Customers/clients are increasingly more in control of a firm's strategy - Certain key accounts must be maintained on a much closer level - Strategy implementation is often longer than many product life-cycles

Competitive Influence of Logistics	Features	Effects
Globalization Across all Sectors	- Supplies, raw materials and product components are increasingly outsourced overseas, produced offshore or sourced in distant markets globally	- Supply chains and commodity chains are much longer than in prior eras requiring both increased asset allocation and greater resources - End to end distribution times have increased due to logistics complexities
Negative Pressures on Product Pricing	- Major international competitors across industries are dependent upon low-cost manufacturing and distribution centers globally - Trade related developments such as reduced barriers to trade, market deregulation and trade agreements place downward pressure on prices - Internet sourcing capabilities result in global price deflation - Globally, consumers are more value-conscious	- Costs must be lowered in order to meet the downward pressure on prices - Less value must be carried within the supply chain; i.e. inventories must be reduced in all supply chain nodes and especially those in close proximity to the end-consumer

Competitive Influence of Logistics	Features	Effects
Customers taking control	- More demanding, not just of product quality, but also of service	- Service excellence can only be achieved through a closely integrated logistics strategy

Clearly, based on the points included within the table above, the supply chain and logistics industry as a whole has become a central competitive pillar. These competitive pillars fall within a firm's capacity to remain relevant within those markets that it competes in.

One of the more pertinent elements mentioned in this synopsis of the logistics field on global competitiveness is that of downward pressure on pricing. The effect is such that the supply chain is often seen as being the only domain in which the downward pressure on pricing can be effectively responded to by globally focused firms. Hence, Saudi Arabia, in developing its economic cities and implementing the Vision 2030 guidelines, recognizes that economic stability cannot be assured when the national economy is dependent upon, largely, a single source of revenue. This is a single source of revenue which, in this case, is petroleum and petroleum related products and services. In large part, this economic diversification that lies at the heart of the Vision is dependent upon the establishment of the Kingdom's key economic centers which are Jazan, King Abdullah Economic City and several other smaller ones. Yet, these economic centers within the Kingdom will not and cannot be as effective as they need to be without the adoption of international best practices within the logistics field.

The point is emphasized throughout this text that the Crown Prince Mohammad is not content to have Saudi Arabia be merely a regional powerhouse as the nation currently is. Rather, the Crown Prince seeks to give the country the international stature that it deserves as a socio-economic engine within the Muslim world. In order to better affect this vision through the identification and comprehension of cutting edge technologies, improved operations and best practices implementation in areas such as the logistics field is vital to achieving the Vision 2030. In order to assist the Kingdom in achieving these outcomes, this text has attempted to identify the most important of these logistics innovations that are changing the way that business is being transacted in the global marketplace. The most important logistics innovations that can positively affect forward motion with respect to the Vision have been identified as being worthy of discussion in this text. The top 10 logistics innovations then that form this text's chapters are: 1) drone delivery solutions, 2) the use of autonomous freight shuttles, 3) improved RFID chip technologies, 4) digital markers for retail products, 5) wearable technology for workers, 6) traditional postal services, 7) sustainability standards for supply chains, 8) operationalization of the internet for warehousing functions, 9) robotic fulfillment solutions, and 10) self-driving vehicles. All of these core innovations discussed within this text's chapters are and will continue to significantly influence the field. These top 10 innovations in the logistics field have the potential to act as core drivers for the Kingdom's Vision 2030 objectives and that is the argument maintained throughout this book.

List of Abbreviations

3PL – Third Party Logistics
4PL – Fourth Party Logistics
ABC – Activity Based Costing
ABF – Account Based Forecasting
ABM – Activity Based Management
AOM – Advanced Order Management
API – Application Program Interface
APS – Advanced Planning System
ATO – Assembled to Order
ATP – Available to Promise
B2B – Business to Business
B2C – Business to Consumer
BOL – Bill of Lading
BOM – Bill of Materials
BPR – Business Process Reengineering
CBU – Complete Business Unit
CKD – Complete Knocked Down
CMI – Co-Managed Inventory
COGS – Cost of Goods Sold
CPFR – Collaborative Planning and Forecasting Replenishment
CRM – Customer Relationship Management
CRP – Capacity Requirements Planning
DRP – Distribution Resources Planning
ECR – Efficient Customer Response
EDI – Electronic Data Interchange
EOQ – Economic Order Quantity

ERP – Enterprise Resource Planning
FAK – Freight All Kinds
FEFO – First Expire First Out
FIFO – First in First Out
FMCG – Fast Moving Consumer Goods
FOB – Free On Board
FSI – Free Standing Insert
FTL – Full Truckload
FTZ – Free Trade Zone
GPS – Global Positioning System
GVW – Gross Vehicle Weight
JIT – Just-In-Time
LIFO – Last In First Out
LO/LO – Lift-on/Lift-off
LTL – Less than Truckload
MAPE – Mean Absolute Percent Error
MPS – Master Production Schedule
MRO – Material Repair and Overhaul
MRP – Material Requirement Planning
MTD – Month to Date
NIFO – Next In First Out
NVOCC – Non-Vessel Operating Common Carriers
OEM – Original Equipment Manufacturer
OFS – Oil Field Services
OMS – Order Management System
OS&D – Over, short and damaged
PO – Purchase Order
POP – Point of Purchase
POS – Point of Sale
POD – Point of Delivery
POE – Point of Entry
QR – Quick Response
RFID – Radio Frequency Identification
RMR – Retail Management Replenishment
RTV – Retail Management Replenishment
SCE – Supply Chain Execution

SCM – Supply Chain Management

SCP – Supply Chain Planning

SKU – Stock-Keeping Unit

SMI – Supplier Managed Inventory

SRM – Supplier Relationship Management

TMS – Transportation Management System

TOFC – Trailer on Flatcar

TQM – Total Quality Management

UFC – Uniform Freight Classification

VMI – Vendor Managed Inventory

WIP – Work in Process

WMS – Warehouse Management System

YTD – Year to Date

CHAPTER I
Invasion of the Drones

The thought of drones populating the skies and performing what are now largely viewed as mundane tasks is still an amazing thing to consider. Yet, it seems that the future is indeed here because drones are populating the skies and performing very mundane tasks from surveying to package delivery and all things in between. Drones or what are sometimes referred to as unmanned aerial vehicles (UAVs) seem to have invaded every aspect of human existence over the past several years. Of course they have become hugely successful on the retail side where many hobbyists and people from various professions such as photography to real estate have adopted the technology. Fields as diverse as construction engineering, civil inspections and so on have utilized drone technology to undertake inspections of bridges and other large structures that previously would have been very difficult to inspect on a regular basis. However, despite the high visibility of drones in these various segments and industries, it is the logistics and supply chain field where drones are having a much more pervasive impact.

The logistics field has recognized in drone technology a means to gain efficiencies that would otherwise be impossible to achieve. Logistics and supply chain management are activities that are especially dependent on the element of achieved efficiencies. This is because one single inefficiency anywhere upstream or downstream in the process of moving goods and products typically has a magnified effect elsewhere within the supply chain. Hence, drones are a major technological development that is targeted almost specifically at the issue of efficiencies that can be gained and this is why they are so relevant to supply chain management(note a). For example, companies such as Amazon are integrating drone technology in order to expand, enhance or complete their supply chains. These developments are found within a range of fulfillment centers where drones are used to retrieve certain hard to reach or hard to find items. This mobility in turn allows such facilities to reduce the mechanization required to move human workers about the facilities.

Reducing or removing this type of mechanization facilitates the reduction of human interaction with the goods and materials that populate the supply chain. Thus, the outcome is the automation of the entire fulfillment process even further. Drones are, by definition, fully automated vehicles that when in specialized form, are able to one task very efficiently with little maintenance, no oversight and reduced cost. This is because of their capacity to travel to remote or out of the way areas within spatially large and diverse structures. These structures being those that constitute major operational centers of any supply chain such as warehouses and so forth as the image below indicates:

Figure 1: Delivery Drone

The picture demonstrates that a drone is not dependent upon fixed transportation routes within a facility and can bypass or go over impediments to smooth product movement. Also, such developments can be found in the actual supply chain vis-à-vis product movement and transportation. This development is evident where drones are being developed to complete the proverbial "first mile" and "last mile" for products from production facilities to local distribution centers. It is these first mile and last mile elements within the typical supply chain that pose the most significant and therefore costly elements within a supply chain because the infrastructure to service these elements is costly with a relatively small percentage of the overall returns. In turn, drones are being used to move these same products from local distribution centers to the consumers' homes or the end-user's place of business as the case may be.

Much of this innovation in the logistics field is due to the shift in retail from bricks and mortar to online venues. It is clear that retail is increasingly shifting to online sales platform considering the glut of retail bankruptcies occurring worldwide. As Amazon in the United States and Taobao in China continue to expend the number of product lines and services that they are involved in, traditional retailers such as Carrefour and Walmart are all faced with developing online sales channels or becoming essentially irrelevant. In the online space, online retailers are now offering a range of purchase options which depend upon extreme flexibility within the delivery modality of the product. Drones fulfill this extreme delivery flexibility because they are both adaptive as well as inexpensive, comparatively speaking, which makes them especially attractive to retailers who function off of incredibly thin margins to begin with. Drone delivery has applications to a range of activities within the traditional retail supply chain. This range of activities are those including new products and services as well as secondary applications such as new product returns with damage, product exchanges and used product returns for warranty service or similar among other applications. These activities all depend on, at some point, logistics processes that can or could be met through drone related applications.

Additionally, many online retailers are finding that they must also offer a range of shipping options as well which can, more and more, also be met through drone technologies in the marketplace. In fact, major online retailers are almost all experimenting with innovative new shipment solutions such as drones, same-day delivery with traditional shippers and contract drivers through Uber and other similar solutions. However, drones are currently capturing the fancy of many of these online retailers because of their low cost, scalability and granular delivery options. Increasingly, online purchases are rapidly evolving into a viable alternative for all consumers rather than just those consumers who are comfortable in the online environment. Consequently, the retailers and businesses that support emergent online processes must reflect on how to apply these new disruptive developments such as drone technology. The current and emergent online retailing platform must consider how drone technology could streamline delivery processes. This logistics component must be seamless and allow the consumer to control the feedback and input processes as well. In sum, drone technology for the online retailer must provide adequate choices for shipping and delivery or consumers may opt for another online retailer that does offer such alternatives.

It is apparent that drones are now being developed that can improve a host of different transportation related activities. For instance, some drone applications can now assist with traffic flows in congested urban areas such as bridges, intersections and so forth because they can provide what amounts to dense, real-time data about where traffic is bottle-necking (see note b). The result is that traffic flow within the supply chain has the potential to become much more efficient, effective and transparent up and down the supply chain. In essence, rather than being stuck on fixed routes, the supply chain would have the capacity to become more fluid based on real-time traffic patterns. Drones by nature are able to overfly congestion in a manner than no other delivery modality can achieve for physical products and items. Yet, they also serve to shift online ordering and delivery from a planned purchase behavior in the consumer to what amounts to an impulse buy in some sense. This is because drones ensure that a consumer can make an impulse purchase with the expectation that the impulse will be gratified in a much shorter timeframe than would otherwise be the case. Furthermore, drones are also being developed as a means to deliver supplies, materials and equipment to seagoing vessels as well as to undertake marine surveying activities for inspections and monitoring purposes.[2] These vessels are typically located in remote or isolated ocean-going environments that are difficult or expensive to service.

4

Drones can provide what amounts to a low-cost method to assist sea-going vessels with resupplying in-between more comprehensive servicing requirements. In relation to the Vision then, drones provide an actionable technology that is inexpensive, widely available and already market tested as a means to improve or extend existing supply chains. Basically, the Kingdom's economic centers would not need to invest the resources to develop their own unique drone platforms from the ground up. Instead, they build off of the success of newly emergent drone technologies currently in use and currently in development:

Figure 2: Warehouse Drone

Such technologies have the ability to immediately develop efficient fulfillment and inventorying facilities. As the image above demonstrates, drones can navigate aisles even while these aisles are occupied by other logistics resources. These advantages achieved through drone technology, in turn, are very attractive to international investors and companies intent on positioning themselves within the Middle East marketplace. Since certain elements within the Saudi Vision 2030 such as the series of economic cities underdevelopment like King Abdullah Economic City and its King Abdullah Port, include multimodal transportation facilities, drone technologies are vital to their efficiency.

Drones are what might be described as the ultimate in granular delivery solutions. For many retailers, the logistics of managing same-day delivery is much simpler to manage if one has the alternative to utilize drones to make many of the smaller deliveries that come in throughout a given 24 hour period. Same-day delivery services are now being offered by many, if not most, major retailers both on-ground and online which is a movement being led by Amazon. For instance, even major on-ground, traditional retailers like Macy's in the US now offer same-day delivery options for many of their products. The point is that even traditional retailers have had to ensure that they can make many more of the consumer product goods that they sell and market available online through their websites. In this regard, drone technology is one of the logistics solutions that can make a traditional on-ground retailer also a successful online retailer. The use of drones enables this option as a means to facilitate the same day delivery that so many consumers now prefer. In order to attract these consumers and placate their need for immediacy and immediate gratification, same-day delivery is fast becoming an expected option. Without such a same-day delivery option, consumers may not make the purchase decision based on the extremely low price-points that are achievable in the online environment versus the on-ground environment. Drones facilitate these strategies for many retailers but do so solely within the context of the logistics function.

One of the primary drivers for drone applications within the logistics industry is the same-day and next-day delivery modalities. The fact is that same-day and next-day delivery solutions within the supply chain is vital to any firm that expects to be able to compete in the contemporary retail space whether online or on-ground. Of course, a retailer always has these options now but they are not as granular in character as they are with drone technology. Presently, drone deliveries within the supply chain is also accompanied with a high degree of novelty which certainly adds to the attraction. Those retailers that do manage to integrate drone technology into their retail supply chains can expect to benefit financially from increased purchases in the short term. This outcome is just because of the novelty factor as consumers make purchases just to see their products delivered by drone. These types of delivery modalities are part of the developing omnichannel retail paradigm.

Within the traditional distribution center logistics framework is one that is not conducive to how consumption in the marketplace is currently being supported by major online retailers such as Amazon and other retailers building out major online presences. The fact is that fulfilling demand within the emergent omnichannel and its emphasis same-day and next-day delivery modalities is difficult within the context of the traditional fixed route delivery process. It is evident that a fundamental reconceptualization of the entire distribution channel that shifts away from the heavy reliance on distribution centers to a model based more on actual in-store fulfillment is required for contemporary retailers. The omnichannel is a direct-to-consumer channel that leverages all of the available inventorying nodes possible along a supply chain which includes the traditional retail establishment itself. Within this context, retail stores are in the best position to function as what amount to inventorying nodes for drone-based delivery models within a given community. This is because these retail stores already exist within the communities into which drones are being sent to complete the last mile delivery solutions for individual logistics applications. In this regard, it should be noted that same-day and next-day fulfillment of many if not most retail products do not work well in the context of a traditional supply chain paradigm.

In order to remain competitive over the past several years, many retailers who seek to market a rapid fulfillment of products/services to consumers must first invest in their supply chain and logistics channels. These adaptive retail omnichannels relying on innovative solutions such as drones demand an investment in the supply chain and logistics operations. In many instances, such logistics solutions can best be offered by 3rd party providers for the same-day/next-day delivery of products.[3] Yet, even outsourcing such drone delivery models from 3rd party provides still requires system changes in the logistics design of a given retailer. This is because the products still must be delivered to the given carriers in an efficient manner and then exchanged intermodally to the drone delivery platform.

Figure 3: Omnichannel Retailing Supply Chain

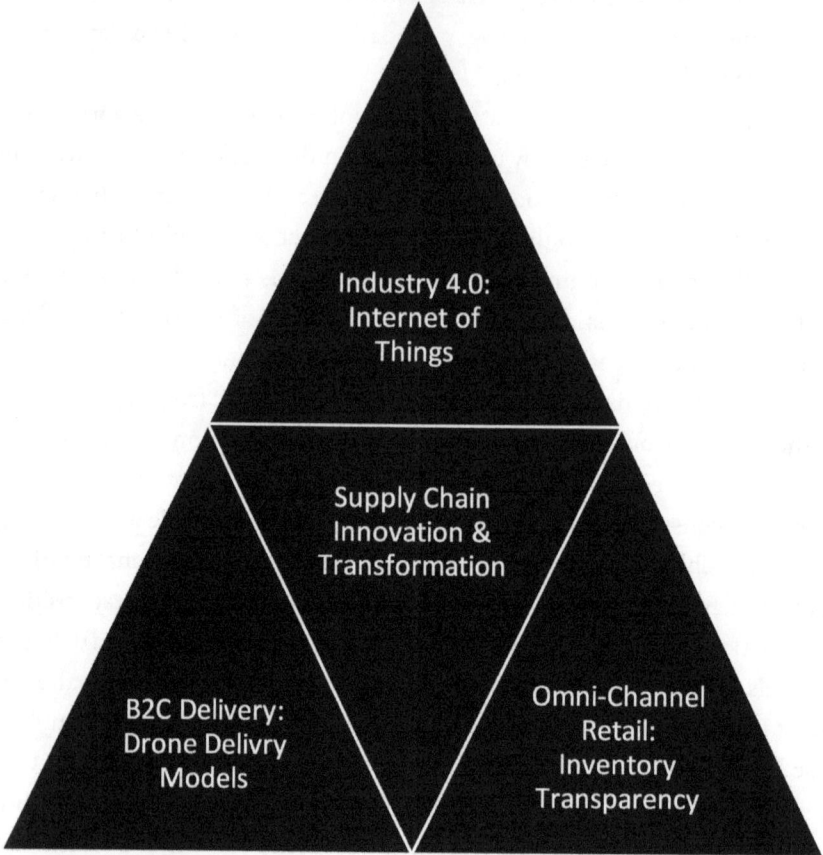

Industry 4.0:
Internet of
Things

Supply Chain
Innovation &
Transformation

B2C Delivery:
Drone Delivry
Models

Omni-Channel
Retail:
Inventory
Transparency

This type of omnichannel forces producers and retailers to rethink where their product inventories are held. This is why, increasingly, it is the retail outlets themselves that are now seen as key distribution centers given their granular placement within the communities in which the consumer lives. Once producers and retailers are able to make this type of conceptual translation in development of their retail business models, both as distribution centers as well as a shopping center, then the extension of the supply chain using drones becomes very achievable. Such retail outlets simultaneously functioning as distribution centers are key in the establishment of the last-mile extension of the supply chain from the retailer to the consumer's front door utilizing drone-based delivery methods.

The concept of drone-based delivery as a logistics application first entered mainstream supply chain management through Amazon. It was when Amazon announced it was developing its own in-house drone-delivery system.[4] Amazon is an online retailer that has historically been a first-mover with respect to the many technology systems that it has pioneered over the years. Consequently, this drone initiative, while quite radical on the surface, is actually in line with Amazon's technologically focused history of innovation. Amazon's drone-delivery model is referred to by the company itself as Amazon PrimeAir. As such, PrimeAir is a logistics system designed to deliver packages to consumers in 30 minutes or less within those urbanized markets that are targeted by the drone system. Although there are existing drone-based delivery systems available, Amazon decided not to apply an off the shelf drone system due to its own unique and highly specialized needs and applications. Amazon's internal operations are so automated and so unique to the firm that a custom application developed for its supply chain is not simply more efficient but actually required given its logistical complexity. Amazon's executive leadership led by Jeff Bezos recognized this custom need for the company's applications and thus either constantly invested in the development of new technologies or simply purchased companies that had already worked on such technology and invested heavily in it.

Thus, Amazon relied on its own research and development division which designed a purpose-built drone solution tailored to its unique fulfillment processes in its localized inventory centers. The development of a purpose-built drone platform within a complex supply chain like Amazon's allows the technology to truly flourish in a way that would be difficult to achieve with an off-the-shelf system. The company's particular purpose-built drone delivery platform is unique both from a form factor perspective as well as from a system perspective. The delivery of items to consumers in their communities requires a drone platform that is extremely robust compared to the drone applications on the market today in retail format. Retail drones may be sophisticated but they lack the capacity to navigate real-world environments multiple times a day in inclement weather with minimal or no human oversight or supervision. PrimeAir is designed from the ground up to be able to achieve the types of efficiencies and consumer satisfaction outcomes necessary with Amazon's same-day delivery modalities:

Figure 4: Amazon's Drone Delivery Service

The drone pictured above demonstrates the way in which Amazon developed the platform to respond to its need for modularity in order to carry its packages. The company's drone technology is, at its core, fundamentally the same as other drone platforms currently in use, its application is completely unique to the company's functional purpose. The company's drone platform is designed to deliver product packages that weigh as much as 5 pounds within an estimated 30 minute period of time. This type of punctuality and resource scheduling requires the development of localized inventory centers. Amazon's drones are all ted to fly at an altitude of 400 feet or less and to weight no more than 55 pounds each. Furthermore, the operating software for these drones operates on a detect and avoid basis.

The firm's overall emphasis is on identifying how fast the firm's products can be delivered to the consumer following the placement of the order. The faster the delivery to the consumer the more likely the consumer is to continue shopping at Amazon as opposed to a traditional, on-ground retailer. In the final analysis, it is apparent that drone technology is hardly cut and dried as it were. The sheer variety of drone platforms and different form factors ensure that selecting drone applications for Saudi Arabia's rapidly developing economic centers at the backbone of the Vision 2030 requires extensive planning. However, the form factors most relevant to the Vision and the Saudi logistics requirements involve four general form factors. These form factors for drone applications consist of the following categories:[5]

Figure 5: Drone Form Factors

1. Fixed-Wing Drones:

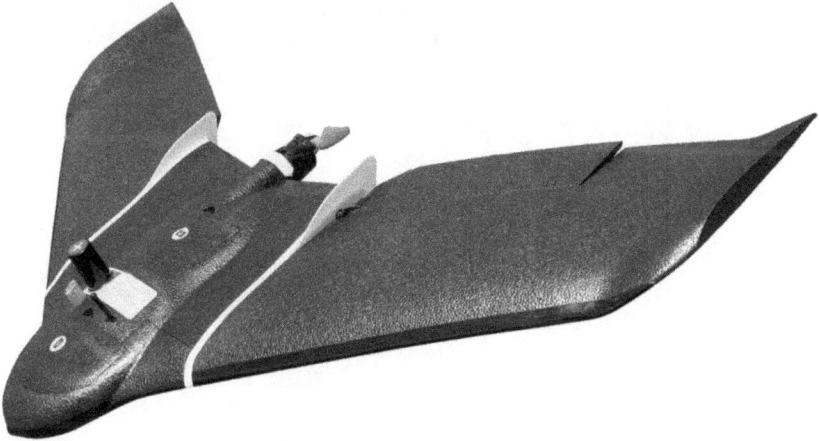

2. Tilt-Wing Drones:

3. Unmanned Helicopter Drones:

4. Unmanned Multicopter Drones:

All of these competing platforms offer their strengths and weaknesses and advantages and disadvantages. The important factor that must be considered for Saudi Arabia and the Vision 2030 needs is identifying which one works best within the given environment in which it will be applied.

The Saudi environment in and around its various economic centers including King Abdullah Economic City, Jazan Economic City, Prince Abdulaziz Bin Mousaed Economic City and Medina Knowledge Economic City all have slightly different environmental elements. For instance, Jazan Economic City sits adjacent to the Red Sea and thus drones intended for outside transportation applications must be able to withstand both moisture and sand in addition to the extreme heat. Likewise, economic centers such as King Abdullah Economic City have a much larger footprint requiring longer periods of sustained flight in and around its fixed structures. Consequently, the particular traits of the different drone form factors must be identified in advance:

Table 2: Drone Form Factor Characteristics

Drone Form Factors	Advantages	Disadvantages
Fixed Wing Drones	* Longer flight ranges * Vehicle stability and durability	* Requires a horizontal take-off (longer take-off/landing requirements) * Reduced mobility while in air
Tilt Wing Drones	* Has both long-range durability and vertical take-off capabilities	* Sophisticated, high maintenance technology * More expensive to maintain and operate

Drone Form Factors	Advantages	Disadvantages
Unmanned Helicopter Drones	* Vertical take-off and flight capabilities * Highly maneuverable while in flight * Larger payloads in flight	* More expensive than fixed wing drones * Higher maintenance requirements
Multicopter Drones	* Relatively inexpensive * Simple launch procedures * Lower weight	* Reduced payload capacities * Susceptibility to high wind velocities

As these descriptions indicate, there are extensive choices for drone applications within the logistics field. These are further complicated by the great diversity of manufacturers of drone solutions in the marketplace. Thus, the different city administrations and industry leaders within Saudi Arabia's economic cities must source a strong industry partner in order to develop their drone infrastructure. These international drone technology developers are increasing in number and are readily available to those entities desiring to adopt such technology within the supply chain.

Consequently, an examination of these different benefits and advantages associated with the competing drone platforms implies that either the helicopter or multicopter platform would be the most appropriate solution within the Kingdom's economic cities. This is because the longer take-off/landing facility requirements of fixed wing drones disqualifies them from high density population areas as well as interior applications within warehouses, storage facilities and multimodal centers. Additionally, helicopter and multicopter platforms have inherently higher load capacities which improve their cost-benefit equation in real-world applications. Logistics applications have to generate economies of scale in order to reduce the overall cost of transportation and movement for a logistics operator on a per unit basis. This per unit costing equation model is diagrammed in the following section:[6]

Figure 6: Cost Equation Model

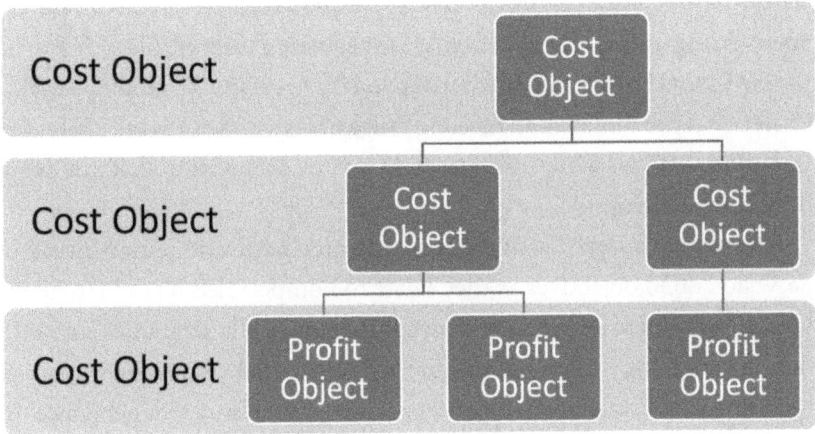

As the above per-unit logistics costing model demonstrates, every time a unit or objective is touched it adds to the cost of transportation. In this regard, a host of ancillary factors must then be included in the cost equation to identify how a particular logistics application such as drone technology can reduce the overall cost of supply chain management (SCM) processes for any given product. This cost equation is included below:

$$C_{cok} = C_{pk} + \sum_i C_{SCOi} \frac{P_{cons_{ki}}}{P_{SCOi}} = C_{pk} + \sum_i C_{SCOi} P_{ki}$$

The cost equation then by which drone technology can be quantified in terms of logistics cost savings includes the following elements:

1. C_{cok} : the overall cost of each unit
2. C_{pk} : the primary cost of each unit
3. C_{SCOi} : the total cost of managing movement
4. P_{scoi} : the total management efficiency of per unit movement
5. P_{conski} : the cost of resource consumption to achieve per unit movement
6. P_{ki}: the actual end cost of per unit movement

This particular cost equation can be used to determine which drone platform would work best in different application scenarios in the Kingdom. However, regardless of the particular cost equation utilized, identifying the specific factors involved in each application is a necessity. To accomplish this it is necessary to understand the long range objectives within the context of the Vision 2030 vis-à-vis logistics, SCM and transportation that achieving the Vision requires.

Drones are a logistics solution that fit nicely within the framework of the Vision 2030 objectives as they relate to non-petroleum based industry support. In order to join the world's leading countries, best practices in world leading technology solutions within the logistics field is as much a part of the Vision as the stated objective ive to achieve petroleum independence. In order to affect the goals and objectives of the Vision, the Kingdom's rulers and especially the Crown Prince recognize that every key sector within the national economy must develop efficiencies. These efficiencies must not simply match those found in other leading economies but must actually surpass those of the world's leading markets. As the Vision states, the private sector within the Kingdom contributes as much as 40% to national GDP and this type of dependence on a single sector is simply not sustainable in the mid to long-term. The private sector within the Kingdom should be contributing some 70-80% or more to the nation's GDP. Thus, the development of key logistics solutions such as drone applications is an actionable strategy that directly affects this objective ive. In effect, as the Vision states, logistics solutions such as drones are a direct outcome of the Vision's objective ive and is a purely logistics driven solution. The Vision itself states that it intends to, "encourage innovation and competition and remove all obstacles preventing the private sector from playing a larger role in development."[1] Drones are actually one of the most innovative aspects of the global supply chain currently revolutionizing the logistics industry and it is clear that the Kingdom can leverage this technology to its benefit.

One emerging application of drones within the logistics sector that has been targeted for use within the Kingdom and certainly within its economic cities is first and last mile transportation solutions. The supply chain has

---

[1] Saudi Vision 2030. 2017. Saudi Government. Retrieved from: http://vision2030.gov.sa/en/node/60

experienced enormous growth over the past 5-6 decades or so as globalization has become the de facto economic model for the global economy. Logistics companies have been experiencing substantial resource issues in achieving first and last mile transportation solutions for global consumer product goods (CPG) manufacturers, resellers and retailers. This is especially apparent in emerging and developing markets where the highest level of population growth is expected through 2030 which is expected to account for about 90% of global population growth. Hence, as trade, consumer purchases and construction have increased internationally drone delivery of products, supplies and equipment can reduce inner city congestion, environmental pollution and reducing transportation costs.

As with most other emergent technologies, Amazon is not the only major technology driven firm that is developing drone-based delivery solutions for product or supply deliveries. Major technology firms such as Google which has both the expertise and the financial reserves to develop drone applications are in the process of expanding their drone-based solutions. For its part, Google has recently applied for a technology patent in the US which is based on a sophisticated drone-based delivery system for retail products. This drone delivery model is designed to fly to what is described as a local delivery box set-up within a given community that is equipped with infrared beacon transmitters. These infrared beacons basically are what help guide this drone platform into the delivery landing zone. Google's drone solution would then place its package into a receptacle on wheels from which consumers would later arrive to retrieve their packages. It is apparent that this drone system is largely similar to Amazon's own drone-based delivery system which is further along in development. Yet, Google's fundamental business model behind its drone application is remarkably different than Amazon's. Where Amazon's drone-based delivery business model is what amounts to a direct to consumer model, Google's drone-delivery solution is a direct to warehouse and then to the consumer model.[7] Hence, Google's drone-delivery system is not necessarily a last-mile solution since the functional inclusion of another delivery/pick-up modality is required. In this case, Google's drone system still retains what amounts to a warehousing layer within the supply chain system. Yet, what it does achieve is an overall time-to-delivery reduction due to the inclusion of a drone-delivery platform.

It should be noted that, despite the significant advances into drone-based logistics applications for producers and retailers such as Amazon and Google, there remain barriers to their adoption. These are what amount to difficult impediments due to resource requirements, regulatory issues and simple supply chain management procedures. Off the shelf technology actually exists to affect drone-based logistics solutions and thus, technically, any producer or retailer is able to leverage drones in first-mile or last-mile applications. However, the largest impediment to drone deployment is the regulatory and the safety factors that are associated with drone technology and use. Most governments regulate air space and the Kingdom is no exception. Although drones tend to fly at relatively low altitudes, it is still difficult to imagine that drones will be given free-reign to fly pell-mell across any of the Kingdom's economic cities.

Thus, Matternet, which is a drone manufacturing company, describes these deployment issues as technical difficulties. Such technical difficulties are those including battery life and collision avoidance problems combined with regulatory requirements for in-flight operations. Regulatory requirements are still developing as well as national governments grapple with the best approach to managing drone traffic which has been problematic at times to be sure. All of these factors place considerable constraints on full drone deployment by producers and retailers either directly or through a 3rd party provider. Of course first movers in drone technology are all advocating national governments to open their regulatory processes to drone operations but this type of market access is still functionally not available in most leading economies. This presents an enormous opportunity for Saudi Arabia to leapfrog major markets such as the UK and the US.

The use of drones within the logistics field directly affects how consumer goods are both inventories and distributed to the end-user whether consumer or business. Drones are a technology solution that is providing supply chain managers with entirely new sets of tools. These delivery options are those that were previously not possible or, alternatively, cost prohibitive to most producers or retailers. For instance, some analysts now recognize that manufacturing facilities, storage buildings with large yards and other outdoor logistics infrastructure can benefit from the use of drones equipped with additional sensor technologies. These are sensor technologies such as RFID equipped drones that are able to navigate the vast interior spaces of fulfillment centers more efficiently and quickly than human operators.

Furthermore, such drones can also be guided by other technologies such as RFID which can emit near field communication signals informing each drone when it is close to its target product, outside of its intended range or otherwise nearing a potentially harmful objective or environment to its operational parameters.

It is apparent that drones have the potential to become an invaluable tool in the management of supply chains and logistics operations. Their inherent capacity to be operated remotely and autonomously ensures that the logistics field will become much more producer and retailer friendly in the future. These particular benefits to supply chain nodes can even be gained at logistics related facilities that are unique in design or layout due to the needs of a particular industry. This is because drone platforms are often physically small, easy to operate and can hover in the fashion of helicopters. In conclusion, many supply chain and logistics facilities consist of large, expansive interior areas in which products are stacked on multi-layer shelves to great height. This essentially means that some sort of automation and machinery must be utilized to retrieve these products or supplies. Hence, drones can be designed to lift any products not excessively large or heavy from elevated spaces and then deliver them to other supply chain nodes.

CHAPTER II
The Rise of Autonomous Freight Shuttles

Everyone knows that the human capital is, more often than not, one of the most expensive elements of any business including the logistics and supply chain industry. Paying for human workers in terms of salaries, benefits, comp time, days off, sick days, injuries and a litany of other human factors is very expensive. Furthermore, it is often the case that once automation is introduced, not only are these human capital factors removed, operational efficiencies are introduced that further elevate the productivity of the business—logistics or otherwise. Consequently, autonomous processes within the supply chain are not only advantageous from a sustainable competitive advantage perspective but they are vital to simple business survival. Autonomous processes, functions and modalities are not just a source of competitive advantage within the logistics industry anymore. Rather, autonomous processes, whether transportation modality or data related are an absolute necessity. Yet, the true economies of scale that can be achieved within the realm of autonomous modalities involves the use of fixed route solutions such as Freight Shuttle Systems or FSS(see note c). The FSS is one transportation solution that has the potential to eventually lower the cost of CPG movement within a supply chain beyond any solution currently under consideration or planning. Presently, there are no fully operational FSS solutions in use but the FSS itself is being developed by researchers at Texas A&M University in the US where several plans are in place to utilize the FSS for cross-border transportation solutions with Mexico.

Additionally, the movement of freight regionally, nationally and internationally is an extremely expensive and resource dependent activity. This is especially true at railyards, ports and other intermodal transfer points within the logistics supply chain. Essentially, anytime that cargo in any form is physically handled it costs the transporter and therefore the shipper money. Typically, overseas containers arriving at major transfer points such as ports and railyards tend to be transferred intermodally or delivered through the use of trucks. Containers arriving in ports, for example, are loaded one by one onto short haul transportation trucks. Such short haul transportation trucks deliver these overseas containers to railyards or other trucking depots for continued transportation or delivery. This process goes on night and day 24 hours a day, 365 days a year without interruption with the exception of unanticipated issues such as strikes, breakdowns or accidents and so forth.

Intermodal transportation is a logistics and operations concept that refers to multiple forms of transportation. Transportation modes within the typical supply chain involves trucking, shipping as in containerized vessels, air transport and railway transport. Hence, intermodalism is a concept that refers to the use of multiple transportation modes in the movement of products and goods from one point to another within the context of the typical supply chain. Intermodal transportation can involve either two or more of these transportation modes within the same supply chain and, sometimes all of them. This is especially the case when speaking of a commodity chain for instance which consists of the entire interconnected node of movement of a product and all of its component parts from the raw material source to the final CPG application.

In this regard, understanding the mechanisms within intermodalism that relate to how products and goods are transferred from one mode of transport to another can mean the difference between profitability or loss for a given enterprise. This is why logistics and the supply chain have become such an integral part of the global marketplace, global competitiveness and of such a critical importance to the success of the Kingdom's economic cities such as Jazan. Intermodal transportation lies at the heart of the global supply chain and without true intermodal functionality, the logistics and supply chain industry would only be a functional department of major manufacturing firms. Yet, with intermodalism, products are efficiently connected from one market to another in a seamless fashion that allows for incredible cost efficiencies to be achieved:

Figure 7: Intermodal Supply Chain Model

FREIGHT TRANSPORT

Certainly, there remain some nodes of inefficiency or nodes that can be improved but overall intermodalism lies at the heart of globalization. Hence, it is because of intermodal technology, logistics and supply chain operations have become a primary competitive differentiator in the CPG industry and, indeed, across virtually all other industries as well. This is the supportive and facilitative role that logistics and the supply chain sector in general plays for all industries. Intermodal operations spans various operators within the supply chain and logistics industries but they are all dependent upon the same types of technological platforms.

Intermodalism requires a sophisticated grasp of technology applications as well. This also necessitates a sophisticated understanding of how data moves through the supply chain management applications that oversee a supply chain as well. Intermodal transportation and shipping would function within a non-technical space but not as efficiently as intermodalism works with technological applications in place. Intermodal exchange of cargo, containers and materials occurs much more seamlessly when such elements can be virtually tracked from origin to destination. It allows each individual unit being shipped and exchanged to be seen by all constituents of the supply chain. Additionally, the technological facilitation of cargo movement through intermodal gateways speeds up the overall delivery process as well. This is why various issues such as data visibility and real-time data access become all the more critical when developing intermodal supply chain strategies. Intermodal transportation requires efficiencies to be developed at the points of transfer from one transportation mode to another in order to be effective. This is because the existence or development of inefficiencies at these transfer points contributes to product shrinkage or loss and disappearance throughout the supply chain. Furthermore, intermodalism is also one of the core philosophical imperatives within supply chain management because rarely does a product or the raw materials that make a product rely on a single transportation mode.

Logistics managers and logistics management as an institution has shifted dramatically in form. This shift is from the command and control paradigm that focused primarily on a hands-on operational model to an emphasis on more automation within the supply chain. The character and sophistication of technology as a logistics management application, and its widespread availability in the market, has altered not only how logistics management moves products but, in fact, altered the very role of the supply chain manager in contemporary logistics 3rd party providers. While there are many technological innovations such as the FSS solution that have facilitated the typical logistics manager's emphasis on automation, no FSS systems are currently being so widely deployed or hold as much promise as the current list of FSS systems that industries throughout North America and beyond are quickly adopting. The growth and development of FSS systems, such as shuttle packages, have evolved over the last decade to mirror the core competencies of the 3rd party providers that employ them. Through this process they have intrinsically shaped the character of the overall logistics operator and contributed to its underlying efficiency. Major 3rd party logistics firms recognize the benefits of developing FSS type applications in those facilities especially that operate intermodally. Intermodal transportation benefits from a minimization of variation, capacity and supply/demand factors.

Presently, major intermodal stations such as ports and railyards still, in large part, rely on a host of more traditional methods of handling freight. There are still transaction points within these intermodal stations that human interaction is required in order to facilitate the transfer of products from one mode of transportation to another and it is these points that perhaps result in the most opportunity for inefficiencies in the supply chain. That is, these types of intermodal stations basically rely on human-driven processes to exchange rail cars, overseas containers and tractor trailers from one platform to another(see note d). This type of intermodal system antiquated, slow and resource dependent. This antiquated transportation system that moves cargo into and out of ports and other intermodal nodes requires massive amounts of fuel to sustain the vehicles being run 24 hours a day, truck and rail car repairs, and finally a host of drivers and operators to maintain the system. However, this antiquated system is also costly and environmentally damaging as well.[8] These trucks usually spend hours waiting in line to pick up and drop off their containers.

Such idleness for the vehicle and the vehicle operator is extremely inefficient. The drivers are being paid by the hour in most instances and thus this is a huge expense when the trucks are caught in long lines waiting pickup or delivery. Additionally, while in-line these trucks spew diesel exhaust fumes into the atmosphere surrounding the ports and transportation hubs. A sample image of a typical port during any regular day is seen below in which the trucks are backed up into and out of the exit gates either waiting to pick up a container or trying to get out of the port to deliver one:

Figure 8: Port Traffic Jams

This type of congestion is not sustainable even in the short-term. The cost of fuel, damage to the local environment and wear and tear on city infrastructure creates all manner of problems for local municipalities in which port facilities are based.

These FSS solutions, such as shuttle platforms, are designed to facilitate many of the transportation and intermodal processes of an logistics operator's internal value chain. As such, they have the potential to maximize every functional process within a logistics operator. Additionally, they can remove a large percentage of the intuitive commitment required of the typical logistics management structure that makes it, as a supply chain institution, so vital in the contemporary global business environment. Specifically, FSS systems as represented through targeted transportation solutions. These are the solutions like these shuttle systems and they have shifted the emphasis of logistics management's focus from competency execution to a more soft skill type of focus on strategic horizons and similar dimensions. This is because these shuttle systems have the ability to execute on competencies based on FSS specific data they themselves collect and operationalize automatically.[9] FSS solutions such as these shuttle systems tend to automate many of the traditional logistics management roles allowing 3rd party providers to reassign, reassess or remove some managerial positions. This too makes them extremely cost-effective over the long-term.

The result is a need for a logistics-driven transportation solutions that both automates and makes more efficient these fixed route systems. The supply chain depends upon these core transportation nodes in order to route products and materials in mass from major inventorying and stockpiling centers. Hence, the need for new and emergent transportation solutions is derived from a need to action to strategy paradigm in order to affect true change in the logistics industry. This paradigm is fundamentally based on linking the structure of the logistics industry with the marketplace. This linking is accomplished in order to develop a strategy to achieve the desired performance outcomes of the strategic objectives of the logistics industry as a whole. These are the same imperatives that stimulate the Vision 2030 objectives that have been described as supporting the use of robotic platforms, automation and machine intelligence throughout all industries within the Kingdom.[10] The action to strategy paradigm essentially argues that a logistics company or operator in a given market should work to align its core business strategy with the inherent structure of the contextual marketplace in which it operates. Thus, any logistics operator within the Kingdom must become extremely familiar with the objectives of the Saudi Vision 2030 as well as its inherent emphasis on economic diversification and social inclusion.

Current research indicates that FSS solutions and platforms are being widely deployed in the market. Logistics companies of all types have found such investment in FSS related technology to the only effective method to provide the level of services required by international customers as well as to develop the internal efficiencies necessary to expand their domestic markets such as Saudi Arabia with its economic centers and cities. Much of this IT and specifically FSS investment in North America and beyond are on technology applications intended to automate a company's internal processes such as these types of shuttle applications (see note e). Shuttle systems are essentially a rail-way that is operated by a group of software applications that are designed to handle different functional areas within an supply chain route—essentially a fixed route. While it could be argued this in itself is not novel and to an extent the idea of a fixed route combined with a software program designed to enhance the functional processes of a particular node in the supply chain is not necessarily new, shuttle systems are considered central to logistics operators. This vital benefit of FSS in particular relates to the overall effectiveness because of their ability to integrate FSS processes across an entire supply chain. Shuttle systems are so coveted because they free up business resources for other applications within the supply chain. They simplify by removing redundant repositories of data as well as redundant systems and positions throughout the logistics operator's channel responsibilities. The redundant depositories of data are removed because, since the shuttle system is, ideally, fully integrated from an FSS perspective into the operator's existing technology platform. Hence, such FSS systems are able to both pull and manipulate data from a single database with numerous fields. As such, the database in these systems forms the nucleus of an logistics operator's FSS technology infrastructure since they are integrated into the overall IT infrastructure.

In this instance, the inherent structure of the marketplace is in the middle of what can only be described as a transformative state of existence. This is where new technology solutions are constantly being introduced into the market. This transformative technological state involves the shifting of the overall structure of the logistics industry from one of petroleum dependence within the Kingdom to economic independence. Such economic independence is such that it involves a growing multitude of different revenue producing industries. These differing revenue producing industries all rely on the logistics industry in order to function smoothly and cost effectively. In order to accomplish this type of outcome, the Kingdom basically recognizes that the economic framework necessitates what is, in effect, an entirely new approach. This entirely new economic approach is what is summarized in the core principles and directives of the Kingdom's Vision 2030 policy platform which enunciates the need to economic diversity in way that must be operationalized through the logistics field. Economic diversity requires the imposition of an entirely new economic planning mindset by the nation's leaders and its municipal administrators. Indeed, it is this progressive and forward thinking by the Crown Prince that not only resulted in the Saudi Vision 2030 but also that is currently stimulating such innovation within logistics and supply chain industries.

One emergent solution that can fully automate a formerly inefficient transportation process at the Kingdom's port facilities is what has been identified as the FSS. While the FSS remains in a state of early development and deployment it retains much promise to automate the logistics operations at port facilities among other intermodal supply chain nodes such as railyards and truckyards especially. This FSS is designed to automate the container transfer process from ports and railyards and to do so in a cost effective and efficient manner. The FSS consists of a rail-like car that is powered electrically and operated remotely via computer software and is currently being spearheaded by a major university in Texas in the US.[11] The FSS and similar automated transportation solutions can be grafted into existing transportation networks albeit with a cost associated with such outcomes. Of course this type of transportation infrastructure can be expensive because of right-of-way concerns and issues but once achieved the returns associated with the FSS are exponential in character.

The use of FSS applications should be a consideration undertaken by every municipality regardless of the municipality's level of logistics industry development. Logistics is a field and industry that influences virtually every community across the globe. In effect, the FSS is a supply chain transportation solution that benefits from economies of scale with little in the way of escalating cost factors. The FSS consists of fixed vehicles that are designed to travel in predetermined routes over predetermined routes on either railways or roadways and, conceivably, in the future, airways as well.

Figure 9: FSS Prototype Design

Presently, the FSS is almost solely limited conceptually to railways. Such railways can be elevated over existing transportation routes which limit their environmental impact on the surrounding communities in which they must operate. One of the most novel and important elements within the FSS solution is that it removes the single most expensive element within any industrial application which is the cost of human capital. The FSS requires relatively few if any operators with the exception of maintenance personnel that could be used from other existing operations. Once put in place, the FSS is fully automated requiring nothing more than a programmer which would already be a part of the existing logistics firm resources.

The logistics market and specifically the retail industry depends upon such FSS infrastructure as a primary methodology to achieve international performance benchmarks(see note f). Researchers have noted that logistics providers are always searching for IT logistics management solutions after building up their core IT infrastructure and systems of which solutions like FSS depend on.[12] For example, while inventorying requirements may demand certain quantities at billing, issues such as seasonality may result in variations in quantities shipped of which FSS is capable of handling regardless. In years past each of these departments would have maintained separate databases as well as different transportation networks that needed to be maintained independently and periodically reconciled. The load on an logistics operator's resources in such a circumstance is obvious wherein the internal storage capacity of the logistics operator can be doubled due to all the storage space dedicated to various data. Additionally, IT staff within the logistics provider suffer an expanded workload due to maintaining redundant systems as well as backing up all of these various applications and databases. Finally, inventory personnel must be committed to enacting various processes to keep supply in stock. Adequate stock levels work to create a product buffer supply to compensate for any systemic issues during the reordering process with suppliers that, in turn, must be managed by the FSS.

The FSS is a supply chain solution that may be anchored in physical operations and managed through IT oversight but the FSS is a targeted solution that provides any firm with access to operational efficiencies over the long-term. While this fixed route solution is focused on the development of the FSS, any scenario that utilizes fully automated vehicle platforms managed as a part of a firm's IT infrastructure is comparable in functionality and potentiality to the FSS to include automated semi-trucks for instance. Yet, applications like the rail cars in particular operate on a predesigned track that connects various intermodal transfer hubs so that they can be scheduled based on demand. Since no drivers and no fuel is required to run this system, the infrastructure necessary to support the FSS has a low carbon footprint and high economy of scale. The FSS is an automated transportation and logistics system that is zero-emissions, reduces congestion on existing roads, automates delivery times to exact schedules and eliminates use/damage to civil infrastructure among other positive features.[13] While the FSS has a relatively high upfront cost this intermodal transfer technology has a sliding scale reduction in cost the longer it remains in use. For the Jazan City For Primary and Downstream Industries, placing a solution such as the FSS in its port and railyards ensures that it can sustain long-term growth in trade while maintaining the quality of life expectations of the Jazan City For Primary and Downstream Industries residents and workers.

With such solutions, logistics providers as well as other supply chain operators, are able to perform value added services within the framework of the same FSS applications and solutions. With such FSS solutions, current inventories can be maintained in real time and the reordering process is automated because many suppliers' systems are integrated into CPG shuttle systems and simply provide product based upon predetermined inventory levels. This all relates to the inherent need for supply chain optimization consisting of different applications, various production schedules generated by the manufacturer's operations and supply chain capacity. Shuttle systems like the FSS can automatically manage CPG demand with the supplier as a means to offering the best price in the right volume at the right time. Previously such a process would have required a staff of personnel with appropriate logistics management experience to implement this process across an logistics operator. This investment in FSS infrastructure across the spectrum of the entire logistics industry has meant that Logistics companies are becoming more competitive in industries far beyond its comparative advantage in manufacturing and production.

The FSS as a critical logistics infrastructure is characterized by several key advantages. These advantages make the logistics solution extremely attractive at a national level for countries such as Saudi Arabia that are intent on achieving world class proficiencies in different industries. Saudi Arabia has the advantage that it is investing heavily in new economic centers in the form of its economic cities that are designed from the ground up for performance within key targeted industries. This characteristic of bespoke municipal design provides city and industry leaders in these economic centers the advantage of being able to integrate all cutting edge solutions such as the FSS among many others within the logistics and supply chain industries. Specifically, the FSS can be said to offer the following benefits and competitive advantages:

1. The FSS can supplant both truck and rail transportation facilities and processes with the development of a single transportation line
2. The FSS leverages advanced electrical engineering for power identified as Linear Induction Motors which are more efficient that traditional electrical motors

31

3. The FSS system is predicated on established, fixed transportation guideways that cannot be diverted, are fully automated and require little maintenance

4. The FSS transportation lines can be erected over existing roadways or railways reducing their environmental impact and cost requirements

These advantages to the FSS as it is currently being developed are especially attractive to economies like the Kingdom's which are themselves expanding in a concurrent fashion. Saudi Arabia has a youthful population eager to work and be productive and when this population attribute is combined with an enabled industry like the supply chain industry, the result is or should be significant economic activity.

The Kingdom's economic cities such as Jazan and King Abdulla Economic City are ideally suited to have such fixed transportation facilities essentially built-in to their infrastructure as they are still being developed. In addition to the clear logistics efficiencies gained from an FSS in the Kingdom, it also has the ability to achieve another important imperative within the Vision. This lies in the Vision's desire to ensure that the Kingdom's citizens enjoy both a higher quality of life and improved lifestyle within its economic centers(see note g). To this end, the FSS works to prioritize quality of life within those metropolitan areas and municipalities where the FSS is targeted to be deployed. These types of imperatives related to the FSS are seen in the table below:

Table 3: FSS Imperatives

Local Roads & Communities	Taxpaying Individuals & Business	Trucking & Transportation Industries	Shipping & Forwarding Entities	Environmental Concerns
Reduced Traffic Congestion	Reduction in Civil Infrastructure Repairs	More Efficient Business Models	Lower Costs for Shipping	Reduced Environmental Emissions
Improved Roadway Safety	Private Funding Structures/No Cost to Taxpayers	Reduced Transportation Costs	More Reliable Shipping Scheduling & Forecasting	Reduced Noise Pollution

Local Roads & Communities	Taxpaying Individuals & Business	Trucking & Transportation Industries	Shipping & Forwarding Entities	Environmental Concerns
Reduced Emissions & Environmental Pollution	Right of Way Rights Licensing Fees to Local Government	Reduction in Delays & Waste	Reduced Damage Risk for Products/ Materials	Reduction of Industry Carbon Footprint
Improved Economic Activity	Lower Product/ Material Pricing Due to Economies of Scale	Resource Allocation	Additional Connections Between Economic Centers	
Job Creation				

These advantages associated with the FSS would be extremely difficult if not impossible to achieve through alternative means. This makes the FSS not only a desirable logistics solution for the Kingdom but, more importantly, a highly suitable logistics solution for its economic centers.

With the proper FSS in place vast swaths of a logistics operator's functional tasks can be integrated into a single technological application or platform. This enables logistics management to move from a human resource managerial type of process to a logistics mediated solution. The implication being such that much less managerial commitment is need to monitor automated processes than is needed to manage logistics staff. Thus, this FSS system has inadvertently made the logistics operator capable of matching industry factors such as supply, demand and forecasting with a fixed intermodal solution. In fact, most FSS and certainly in the case of shuttle platforms, also incorporate, or have the option to incorporate, the overall logistics IT system. The very act of managing a logistics operator's transportation solutions as a unit is integrated into the shuttle's overall FSS value chain(see note h). Such an arrangement has far reaching implications on the size, focus and variety of logistics departments and employees of a given logistics operator that is seeking international parity. This goal of technological parity has led many logistics industries to spend as much as 15-20% annually of total revenues on their FSS infrastructures in order to bring them on-line.[14] Many FSS applications have the ability to assist or even automate such traditional shipment nodes as succession planning for key intermodal solutions.

CHAPTER III
Improving Decades Old RFID Technology

Radio Frequency Identification or RFID is a decades old technology origi-
nating in its earliest forms during World War II. Rudimentary RFID technology was utilized during World War II by the allies as a means to identify
aircraft in the sky to ground personnel. This early RFID technology was
referred to as IFF transponder technology or Identify Friend or Foe(see note
i). This system utilized a signal sent out to arriving aircraft and those that had
the requisite transponders would generate a return signal which resulted in
a blip on the monitoring radar stations. In this regard, the signal being sent
during this early era of modern technology was not the same as RFID chips
emit today but the concept was entirely the same. At any rate, this is the same
general format upon which RFID chip technology is based today. Typically,
there is a radio frequency signal which is sent out and a return signal from
a corresponding RFID chip is returned to the receiver. The form factor for
these senders and receivers differ greatly from one to another but they all
work in essentially the same exact way:

Figure 10: RFID Form Factors

This type of technology is indicative of a sophisticated supply chain which is now comprised of a highly complex and interconnected series of processes. Within the context of RFID, the form factor of the senders and receivers is actually pretty critical. This is because they are utilized in a range of different scenarios within the logistics field. This includes being placed on case and pallets, within individual unit-items. This use includes, increasingly, use on credit and debit cards now among a variety of other uses and applications both within retail and the supply chain.

These processes are responsible for the movement of products and materials but they are often dependent upon data that must be actively managed. At a fundamental level then, the typical supply chain consists of the various nodes that are actively involved in moving some sort of product or material from the producer to the user or consumer. Additionally, this supply chain also includes, in many instances, a reverse supply chain in which product or material is moved back up the supply chain to the retailer or producer. Thus, in order to understand the importance of RFID to the contemporary supply chain, it is important to understand what the supply chain is and what it is comprised of. Hence, the supply chain can be said to consist of a mix of different producers or manufacturers, transportation operators, fulfillment centers, warehousing and storage facilities, distributors, whole sellers, re-tailers and even the end-users and consumer. These different nodes within the supply chain ideally form a seamless transportation and data network. This transportation and data network is one that is increasingly facilitated through the use and application of various technology platforms such as RFID which both generate useful data and collect it as well.

The observation is such that the typical supply chain is not just facili-tated by the existence of data but rather by the flow of information. This flow of information passes throughout the supply chain and it often essentially mirrors the physical infrastructure of the supply chain in that each node generates its own unique series of data-points. The emphasis on contempo-rary supply chains is one of having and maintaining access to real-time data, data visibility and data compatibility across technology platforms where RFID is one of the chief ways in which product or material data is captured. It is evident that failures, bottlenecks, breakdowns or inefficiencies in any of these areas can, essentially, work to undermine the effectiveness of any supply chain.[15] Lack of or loss of data regardless of how integrated the phys-ical transportation nodes are across a supply chain's various links results in an interruption of supply(see note j). Within this supply chain technology network which depends on the active generation of data, factors such as data visibility and data compatibility are all interrelated. This interrelation of data types, forms and feeds are associated with constantly evolving technologies such as RFID and thus they are critical to the continued development of more efficient logistics operations and supply chains. RFID in particular has had an enormous impact on the logistics and supply chain industry by virtue of its capacity to be fully automated within the supply chain.

RFID works, once in place, without any form of physical interaction with a logistics worker or other resource other than related RFID equipment and devices. RFID signals can be emitted and read without the reliance on other dedicated or scarce resources within the supply chain. In its various current iterations, RFID applications consists of fairly well established technological mechanisms. RFID as a concept refers to the use of a radio emitting computer chip contained in some sort of tag that contains all manner of product or ma-terial information. The chipped tag is typically placed at the case or pallet level that contain products and materials but the overall cost of these RFID chips have dropped so much that many individual products are now inventoried with RFID chips as well. As these RFID enabled products move through the supply chain, all the different nodes have RFID scanners that read the RFID signal being emitted from the products or materials being transported. This data is subsequently uploaded into the logistics technology platform through which the overall supply chain is being managed. RFID itself may be an old technology which was initially developed in order to facilitate the recognition of allied aircraft during World War II but its most recent iterations are extremely sophisticated in form and design.[16] As the scanners pick up data emitted from the different RFID chips, the supply chain becomes informed about factors such as product quantity, issues related to product loss or shrink and product age and so forth. The sheer number of possibilities and applications of RFID within the supply chain ensures that while it is in wide use, its potential within the supply chain remains largely in its infancy as it were.

RFID chips are characterized as being either passive or dynamic. The only distinction with respect to dynamic or passiveness lies in whether or not the RFID chip has its own onboard power source or not. Passive RFID chips do not mean a significant loss in functional utility but rather only means a greater limit on signal range, lifecycle of the RFID chip and the amount of data that can be stored, transmitted and processed. However, regardless of the format, they function in largely the same manner in both forms. Passive RFID implies these chips are powered on by the received signal that is emitted by the RFID reader or scanner. Likewise, dynamic means that the RFID chips have their own onboard and independent power source that automatically broadcasts its own signal. Within the context of supply chain management, RFID technology appears up and down the supply chain as a key logistics technology.

RFID chips are utilized on a global basis as well in which overseas containers and freight cars on trains are tagged with RFID chips which transmit data such as origin, material and delivery data. This allows material firms to engage in downstream logistics activities such as just-in-time or JIT inventorying and similar logistics practices. Thus, the application of RFID technology within the supply chain holds as much promise for industries across the board. Yet, there are ongoing concerns about how to apply the technology most effectively within the context of supply chain management. While this RFID technology was not widely applied in the years after the war, it slowly developed over time resulting in more practical applications of the technology. These applications occurred within a variety of different industries from transportation infrastructure to retailing as well as, eventually, some early adoption across the logistics sector itself.

Therefore, it is evident that some of these more practical uses of RFID solutions began to appear during the 1970s and 1980s. These occurred when RFID transponders were placed on railcars which allowed railway operators to more effectively track their railcars. Also, RFID as a fully autonomous platform was also integrated into many developed nations' toll road systems as a means to facilitate more convenient and faster payment of tolls without necessitating actually stopping to pay for a vehicle. These and similar applications alerted other industries of the potential for RFID use for different applications and subsequently RFID solutions began to be explored in more earnest since then. Presently, RFID chips and related technology appear in various applications such as: 1) tracking of product at the case and pallet levels, 2) integrated into credit card technology, 3) ID tags for pets and animals, 4) the tracking of overseas containers, 5) a host of anti-theft systems in cars, 6) building access technology, and 7) patient and prison inmate monitoring systems(see note k). It seems clear that the full range of potential applications for RFID applications has yet to be fully realized. This is due to the fact that given the continuing improvement of the technology within the logistics field there is a constant stream of innovation within the RFID industry and how it responds to logistics operator requirements.

Additionally, RFID technology itself crosses industries where it is used in many different applications such as charged toll roads and, increasingly, within credit and debit cards and other payment systems. RFID technology has not radically altered in form for many years but the type and amount of data that RFID chips can transmit and collect has grown exponentially in tandem with the sophistication of the underlying technology. Yet, recently, with the onset of factors such as consumer identify theft and problems with material security, certain organizations have begun to develop RFID chips that are hack-proof or secure. These hack-proof chips are able to prevents shrink in the supply chain and the theft of often critical material data from fulfillment centers, warehouse facilities and storage depots. These types of still developing RFID technologies are manufactured with an onboard number generator that produces a new access key with each transponder activation. Simultaneously, the system's central managing server utilizes the same random number generation. Such random number generation is meant to ensure that each RFID transponder activation is also a valid one within the context of the supply chain. Validity of the transponder activation is critical to product shipment and inventory accuracy with respect to forecasting, inventory buffering and order replenishment.

In terms of their actual function, the quality of being either active or passive vis-à-vis the RFID chip makes a huge difference within the supply chain. As previously mentioned, at the heart of all RFID technology and its competing application forms is the RFID chip itself. The RFID chip is what actually contains the radio emitter which emits the system's radio signal which is then interpreted by the programmed logic within the integrated circuit. In this regard, RFID chips are also characterized as transmitters which provide a signal containing information about whatever the RFID chip is associated with within the supply chain. Since, as already observed, a passive RFID chip does not have its own independent power supply but instead are energized externally when they are scanned by an electronic field, their utility is dependent upon a paired scanner. From an operational perspective within the supply chain, it is because passive RFID chips do not contain their own power source that they are also limited in their overall effective operating range. While in previous eras the size of the RFID chip was a direct correlation of its range, this is no longer the case as miniaturization has led to the development of extremely small form factor RFID chips in the marketplace. In many instances, these small form factor chips are simply stick on devices that attach much like tape:

Figure 11: RFID Tape

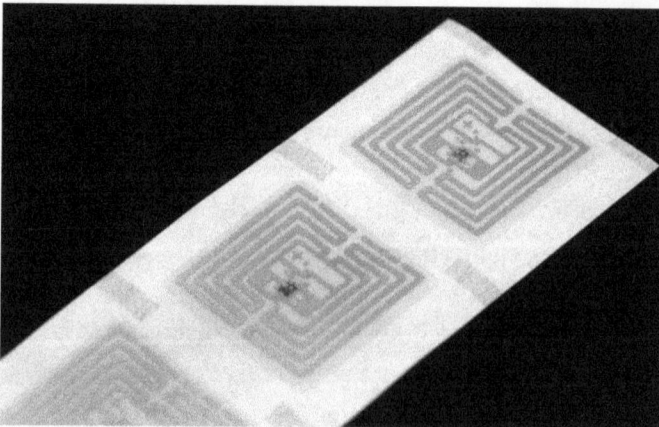

Additionally, the lack of an onboard power source also limits the amount and type of data that the chip can store. Furthermore, unlike their active or dynamic RFID chip counterparts, such passive RFID chips are somewhat limited in terms of their uploading capacity. Uploading capacity equates to the RFID chip's capacity to be written-to or their write-to functionality that allows the supply chain management system to enter new data onto the chip or to update the chip's existing data. These types of characteristics somewhat limit the functionality of the passive RFID chip within the supply chain although they do have their uses. Of course, these limitations also work to ensure that passive RFID chips are cheaper to produce allowing them to be applied over a wider spectrum of materials, products and applications. In many instances, highly sophisticated chips are not necessary for most retail purposes where the signal itself achieves the functional purpose of having the chip in place.

In contrast to their passive counterparts, active RFID chips provide much more functionality and operational use. For the supply chain that is interested in deploying the technology, dynamic RFID chips come in many different forms. Active RFID chips have the ability to greatly enhance a supply chain's effectiveness at moving products from one node to another and at achieving a cost-benefit on a per-unit basis. Active RFID chips are equipped with their own independent power supply in the form of an on-board battery as well as their own transmitting antennas. This onboard power source and antenna ensures that the chip is capable of transmitting its data over much longer distances than passive chips and of processing larger amounts of onboard data. Furthermore, active RFID chips can be programmed or written-to much more easily. For some active chips, the data stored within the active RFID chip can reside passively within the chip until it is powered-on by an RFID scanner thus saving power and extending the life of the RFID chip. Clearly these are the types of advantages with respect to the dynamic RFID chip that are sought after when selecting them for use within the supply chain. Although they are gained at a cost, the cost of these types of RFID chips is lowering rapidly. This is allowing them to be deployed within the supply chain at ever more granular levels within the typical logistics operations.

Essentially, the RFID chip and its supporting technology is capable of replacing the functionality and use of the traditional UPC (uniform product code). For many years, the UPC has formed an important data function within the supply chain from the manufacturer to the end-user or consumer. RFID chips can contain all of the information that the traditional UPC does and much, much more besides. Where the traditional UPC code contains only the most basic product data such as what the product is, when it was manufactured and its per unit cost, the RFID chip can contain this information and more. This includes relevant data like expiration dates, the specific date and time the product moved through any node within the supply chain, the product's overall manufacturing cost, its retail price, and even component part data. All of this data has a purpose which in previous eras was collected and managed through the use of several different methodologies and technologies such as the traditional UPC sticker and concomitant scanners that read them. This wealth of data and information on a given material or product holds much promise in terms of enhancing the efficiency of logistics operations. A supply chain is a process of co-dependent elements that all must collaborate in a meaningful way in order to preserve the integrity of the system. Also, RFID chips are ideal for implementing a more seamless closed loop supply chain which is one that accurately redirects products/materials back for recycling or refurbishment.

RFID technology and its supporting applications have been implemented across a wide spectrum of industries from retailing to government contracting to those such as the pharmaceutical industry. These industries have all recognized the important utility that RFID chips provide. Within the context of the supply chain, RFID chips improve inventory management and forecasting, reduce product shrinkage and enhance data visibility within the supply chain. In order to ensure that RFID applications are effective and to make them work appropriately, logistics firms must also have the capacity to deploy or develop the underlying technology platforms that RFID chips and the data that they generate. One noted early adopter of RFID technology is Wal-Mart. In 2003 Wal-Mart began implementing an RFID enabled supply chain application and went on to require that virtually all of its suppliers and vendors begin tagging all products at the case and pallet level with RFID chips by 2005.[17] The outcome was such that it resulted in more accurate product inventory levels as well as reduced product shrinkage due to theft, spoilage and loss. The benefits to Wal-Mart of its RFID strategy were almost immediately realized. This is because Wal-Mart's RFID enabled supply chain became more responsive to product inventory levels on the shelf in its retail outlets. This in turn allowed its suppliers to replenish inventories faster than might otherwise have been the case without them. The long-term result for retailers that use RFID to manage their supply chains is ultimately more satisfied consumers. These consumers do not have to take a rain check in order to get a product that the retailer might have advertised but subsequently ran out of because of unexpected or unforeseen demand.

Other applications for RFID technology are found industries as diverse as the defense contracting industry. The defense contracting industry is an industry that has multiple layers of contractors, sub-contractors as well as government agencies that must all coordinate at multiple levels of operations. These logistics operations include product/supply ordering, product/supply storage and product/supply transportation according to very strict government regulations. In the US, RFID technology was initially mandated within the Department of Defense or DOD during 2003 when the department required its largest 100 suppliers to implement RFID tracking technology for all of their case and pallet products/supplies as well as for all high-cost/high-dollar items.[18] Initially, this level of RFID tracking at the case and pallet level was sufficient in appeasing the needs of the logistics industry but mostly of the major CPG retailers. Retailers such as Walmart relied on these technologies and RFID in particular as a means to develop a sustainable competitive advantage in the marketplace. RFID supported the ability of suppliers to achieve lower operating costs and which allowed them to pass these lower operating costs onto the retailer which in turn passed lower costs onto the consumers.

This particular RFID strategy ensured that the US's major defense contractors which includes firms such as Boeing, Raytheon and Lockheed Martin, among others, would develop world-class competencies RFID solutions. These RFID solutions could then be benchmarked by logistics firms outside of the defense contracting industry to allow them to benefit from the technology's ability to operationalize the supply chain. This is because large corporations such as these types of defense contractors have the research and development (R&D) dollars to develop and deploy cutting edge technology solutions. Once developed, these solutions can then be adopted at lower costs by other industries. The end result is in a constant cycle of technology transference in which once a technology leaves the military and defense complex and is applied within the private sector, significant advances are made to the technology. New and innovative uses for the technology are created that were never conceived of by the technology's original developers and such is the case with RFID. The current list of potential applications of RFID in the logistics and supply chain industries is long but the possible applications of the technology continues to grow despite its relative age.

The pharmaceutical industry is another major industry that seems to have immediately recognized the importance and competitive advantage that RFID technology offered. The industry was in part spurred on by the US's Food and Drug Administration or the FDA to undertake meaningful feasibility research on the use and application of RFID tagged pharmaceutical products.[19] The intention for pharmaceutical firms was to reduce the possibility of pharmaceutical theft and to improve the prescription process within the medical community. Thus, RFID chips within the pharmaceutical industry have received a great deal of developmental attention with ever increasing miniaturization, disposability and encrypting being much of the industry's focus across the board. The image below demonstrates just how small RFID chips can be within the pharmaceutical and other industries that use the technology:

Figure 12: Small RFID Chip

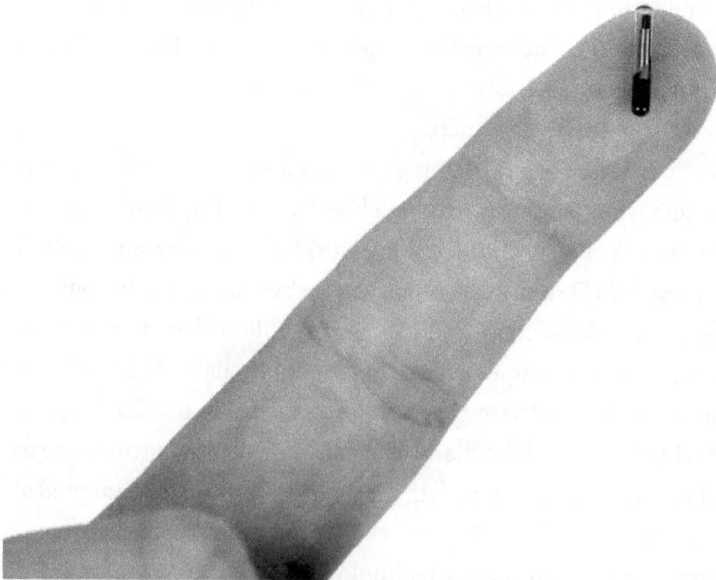

As a result, major pharmaceutical firms such as Bristol Meyers Squib have managed to place RFID tags on all of its pharmaceutical products. These RFID chips on all pharmaceutical products is managed from manufacturer to the pharmacy or hospital distribution point which then allows both the manufacturer and the distributor to more accurately monitor the scripting activity of valuable or commonly abused prescription drugs. Thus, the RFID chip on pharmaceutical shipments contains important data that is tracked within the supply chain. This is data that includes data-points like component ingredients, the drug date and time of production, drug expiration dates, qualifying medical uses for each drug and approved off-label applications.

At the center of the RFID technology enabled supply chain is a centrally developed and managed set of standards. These standards are those that firms must adhere to in order to achieve the full benefit of RFID solutions within the supply chain. Presently, RFID supply chain technology standards are overseen by a firm identified as EPCglobal.[20] EPCglobal has worked to develop what amounts to a universal set of standards for RFID technology. These standards apply to RFID chips that operate between 125KHz to 2.45GHz in frequency, standard RFID chip scanners and the development of a functional model of operation within the supply chain based on what is identified as the EPC or electronic product code.

This is the type of empirical paradigm that is designed and standardized across industry as means apply RFID technology in a universal manner. EPCglobal has created or advocates for an RFID platform that effectively replaces a number of individual components within the traditional supply chain. These are essential supply chain components such as the traditional UPC code which is associated just with a single technology application seen in the bar code and bar code scanner. Only so much information can be included in this bar code format is thus it is limited as to the overall utility of the system for improving supply chain operations. EPCglobal's standardized RFID system is based on the following core elements:

1. The EPC or the electronic product code itself which is nothing but a uniquely generated number assigned to any product within a given supply chain application
2. The overall ID System which encompasses a supply chain's RFID chips and supporting RFID scanners

3. The EPC Middleware application which is the software that interprets the RFID data that is scanned from an RFID chip and then delivers it to the host supply chain management application

4. Product Discovery Services which is an EPCglobal maintained network to which firms subscribe that allows the firms' supply chains to achieve visibility of any product data in EPCglobal's system with the appropriate system permissions

5. EPC Information Services or the EPS IS which facilitates the overall exchange of data and information with any other EPCglobal subscriber across EPCglobal's global network

This type of operational framework is one in which virtually any firm has access to related RFID data. However, the subscribing firms must also have deployed the requisite technology hardware to support an RFID application of their own.

The specific disadvantages and advantages of an RFID solution in terms of functional application within an actual supply chain vary in form, severity and benefit to an implementing firm. RFID enabled supply chains require a network of both hardware and software in order to make use of an RFID technology platform. Among some of the more significant negatives associated with RFID technology with respect to the supply chain is that the RFID signal emitted from the system's RFID chips is susceptible to a great deal of external interference. This interference can originate from existing signals from cell phones, stray microwaves and even other RFID chips and RFID signals. Also, some RFID chips are also susceptible to signal breakdown from proximity to both water or some types of metal. Overcoming these negatives requires the supply chain manager to design these deficiencies out of the overall logistics system entirely. This can be accomplished by ensuring that RFID chips are placed in areas not exposed to water or metal and by limiting the presence and use of other electronic devices in RFID enabled supply chain nodes. However, the advantages of deploying an RFID application within a supply chain, in addition to those already referred to, are that an RFID signal can be read solely through proximity to an RFID reader alone. This RFID scanning is accomplished automatically rather than relying on a handheld scanner or subject to specialized positioning requirements within a logistics network. The conclusion to be taken away from these observations is that supply chain operators benefit from a reduction in manpower necessary to manage product shipment and inventorying.

The potential applications of RFID technology moving forward are numerous. These potential applications have yet to be fully explored. These future or developing RFID solutions include those that involve making closed-loop supply chains more seamless by improving closed-loop supply chain functionality and designing an effective RFID enabled reverse supply chain.[21] The fact remains that product returns and end-of-lifecycle product disposal-recycling amounts to billions of dollars annually across the globe. Clearly, the feasibility of RFID technology capturing lost value contained within product returns and product recycling is recognized within industry the world over but certainly within the Kingdom's economic cities. However, what is lacking within many logistics applications is exactly how to implement a supply chain solution that is efficient enough in managing the reverse supply chain in order to capture this potential value using RFID applications.

In this regard, RFID technology solutions hold the potential to revolutionize this aspect of the typical supply chain. In tandem with existing knowledge regarding the design and management of closed-loop supply chains, RFID technology can be strategically deployed in a way in which not only will the entire supply chain become more efficient but the reverse supply chain nodes can be made more effective. That is effective at making decisions and acting on those decisions in determining how to dispense with products as they move back up the supply chain. Each individual node in the reverse supply chain can make use of RFID technology in order to scan, upload and analyze the data accompanying each product or product component accompanied by an RFID chip. This data and information can then be compared to a predetermined set of decision-making criteria and paired services that accompany each criteria in order to redirect each product or product component to the appropriate node in the reverse supply chain. This is a solution that is not meant to be an off-the-shelf solution per se but rather is one that must be designed for each individual supply chain application because of the variety of end-of-lifecycle outcomes that must be accounted for in each product category. As Saudi Arabia's industrial participants become more focused on sustainability, carbon footprints and green operations, the management of reverse logistics using RFID technology is more critical than ever.

CHAPTER IV
Making Digital Scents

Everyone knows that many industries that were formerly thought to be purely physical based have been converted to a purely digital format. For instance, record stores and books have largely been converted to digital formats which are now largely transactions in cyberspace on the retail side. Yet, even on the back-end of retail operations, many activities formerly thought to be completely dependent on physical interactions have now become digitized. The digitization of entire industries has meant that a slew of processes that formerly required manual intervention have shifted to a completely electronic format. Digitization of various industries is not necessarily a negative and, in many instances, has been a boon for the given industry or led to the development of entirely new industries. What is or what can be negative about digitization of an industry is that such digitization does come accompanied with significant risk of loss in intellectual capital.

Still, digitization has resulted in the emergence of many paradigm shifts across a multitude of industries. Since the logistics and supply chain industries also span a multitude of industries, digitization has a naturally pervasive role to play within the logistics field in general. These paradigm shifts, in turn, have led to the development of entirely new technology formats and platforms necessary to manage the digital processes that oversee such activities. The digitization of such industries as diverse as the music and entertainment industry to the film, camera and video industry has meant that vast swaths of the retail sector have virtually disappeared almost overnight, relatively speaking. This, in turn, has led to just as radical shifts in the formation, design and execution of global supply chains. Since the 1980s and 1990s following the dissolution of the General Agreement on Tariff and Trade or GATT and the adoption of the World Trade Organization (WTO), global trade has expanded exponentially. The WTO has engendered a global trade framework that rewards trade agreements, the free flow of goods and services across borders and provides a platform for conflict mediation. As this trade oriented environment expanded, technology has expanded with it with the result being that producers, distributors and retailers have had to constantly innovate in order to reduce costs in the marketplace.

The mandate for constant cost reduction has meant that all of these participants in the global marketplace have had to innovate on the product development side just to stay in business. Those producers that failed to innovate on the product side have been pushed aside as new product types are pushed onto the global marketplace. Therefore, it should come as no surprise that just several decades ago consumers used to visit record stores to source their music of choice. Alternatively, consumers also once visited book stores to scan the shelves for the most recent bestsellers or hard to find tomes. This ongoing transition to digital form factors and processes especially applies to the logistics and supply chain fields where such digitization typically translates into cost reductions for supply chain operators. For instance, where inventories once required manual counting, visual confirmation and physical checks in order to maintain accuracy, they now are managed almost completely through electronic processes. These electronic processes rely on digitization that works to keep track of inventory levels automatically and even reorder based on these automated counts.

Hence, the digitization within the logistics and supply chain fields has come to require ways to identify products electronically. Within the realm of shrink prevention in the supply chain, inventorying and even counterfeit product reduction all along the global supply chain, being able to delineate one product from another and also one manufacturer from another is vital. This emergence of digital marking or digital scents as it might be described, has been due to the globalization of the manufacturing process for CPGs itself. Hence, one of the more significant issues to emerge within the supply chain and logistics field from the retail side over the past few decades has been counterfeit goods. After China joined the World Trade Organization

(WTO), a glut of counterfeit goods entered international supply chains worldwide (see note 1). China had a major comparative advantage in manufacturing for many years because of its massive labor pool, low wages and decentralized production processes.

Although manufacturing in China was, initially, quite basic, the market's participants quickly identified international best practices. These best practices involved those related to product development, design and manufacturing as a means to elevate its own domestic manufacturing processes. This led to the market's development of a veritable cottage industry in counterfeit products that came to be distributed all over the world in tandem with globalization. Perhaps most shocking, is that for many years the government in China simply looked the other way as this cottage industry in counterfeit goods developed. Eventually, this counterfeit goods cottage industry grew into a sophisticated product development industry in its own right. This counterfeiting industry is one where entire industrial complexes within China began to be dedicated to the production of what are, in effect, nothing more than stolen brands, stolen products and stolen technologies from across the entire spectrum of CPG goods:

Figure 13: Counterfeit Goods in Asia

This image reveals not only the pervasiveness of this counterfeiting industry in China but also the outright brazenness with which it is carried out.

While headway is now being made in undermining the counterfeit goods industry not only in China but other low-cost, low-wage markets as well, it is still a massive global industry that populates the global supply chain with a glut of fake goods. Reducing the glut of counterfeit goods within the supply chain has proven to be a challenging affair and Saudi Arabia wants to take a leading role in eliminating such counterfeit products in the global supply chain. Of course, the Kingdom has a desire to also offer certain competitive advantages to international firms but it wants these to be in the realm of cost efficiencies, intellectual capital and operational factors like competencies in logistics and supply chain operations. To this end, enacting the Vision's principles depends, in part, on deploying certain technology in the supply chain. Such technologies are those that can affect a reduction in counterfeit goods within the nation's supply chain facilities which in turn will work to attract major international competitors to its newly developed economic cities.

The fact is that fake and counterfeit goods are a significant problem the world over now because of the comparative advantage created by low wage, low production cost markets like China. International business, international trade and the global economy all suffer when fake and counterfeit goods are allowed to be sold and marketed as legitimate products. Once these fake goods populate a given supply chain it becomes very difficult to detect them and remove them from the logistics systems. The significance of this issue is apparent in the estimated value of these types of goods which have been put at some US $1.7 trillion which is probably a conservative estimate.[22] Counterfeit goods and products infringe on corporate IP in the form of patent protections, copyright protections and trademark protections. Furthermore, it is not just high-dollar, high-value goods that are being counterfeited by overseas manufacturers. Rather, it is a slew of CPGs ranging from baking soda to computer chips to everyday medicines:

Figure 14: Counterfeit Goods

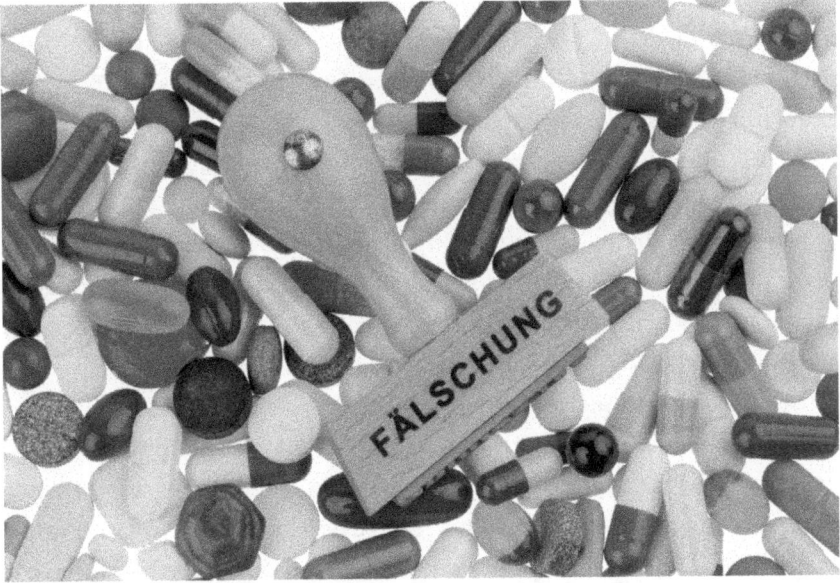

No-one in the west would fail to recognize the similarities between this "Okay" product and packaging and its targeted brand which is "Olay." For consumers located in China and surrounding markets, they simply equate this product with its copied brand and thus the brand is monetarily damaged through this counterfeiting.

There are so many products being systematically counterfeited that it is virtually impossible to source, locate and eradicate all of them. As this image reveals, this company clearly is illegally benefiting financially from all of the R&D, marketing and brand equity that Olay has worked to develop for decades on a global basis. Yet, China is making some progress in tamping down a bit on its counterfeit goods industry. But presently other Asian markets such as Vietnam, Cambodia and Indonesia are now emerging as major counterfeiting markets in which technology designed to reduce or prevent counterfeiting has a significant economic role to play.

As with the Olay (Okay) example, it is apparent that the consumers that this manufacturer markets to are relatively unsophisticated consumers. These consumers simply equate this product with the actual Olay brand shampoos without giving the legitimacy question a second thought. The point is that such counterfeit products can become so commonplace that they actually replace the brand itself in the minds of the consumer. Essentially, those manufacturers that choose to engage in counterfeit product production do so only due to the prior investment made by other firms for legitimate purposes. This is because counterfeiting firms benefit financially from the deep investment that a brand owner has made in core activities such as R&D, product marketing and brand-building as well as in developing a reliable logistics channel and so on. All of these activities require an enormous amount of capital to implement and maintain. Counterfeit firms that piggyback on these investments by other firms merely increase the cost of goods sold for the legitimate producers as well as the final cost of the legitimate goods for the consumers who buy them.

Consequently, fake goods receive all the attention of the original brand but their price does not reflect the true cost of overhead of the original brand. This overhead includes costs such as the development expenses, the costs to market and distribute the product and costs involved in maintaining the brand as well. It is these types of values of fake and counterfeit goods that stimulates manufacturers to produce such goods. Although many of these goods are ultimately manufactured and produced in Asian markets, they can be found in virtually every country and market across the globe. The danger, of course, for the Kingdom and specifically for the Vision is that if such counterfeit products are allowed to enter into the supply chain either targeting the Kingdom directly as a market or passing through as part of the supply chain, international faith in the Kingdom as a place to do business will be undermined.

One still nascent technology that is able to accomplish this is the development of digital product markers. Such digital product markers can be traced throughout the supply chain from producer to retail shelf. The most prevalent form of this digital product marker technology is the use of invisible ink that can be read electronically. One of the leading solutions for the use of invisible ink as a means to combat counterfeit products is being produced by a firm called eApeiron which is located in Miami but that has now partnered with Kodak and Alibaba has established offices in Hong Kong and Shanghai. While the specific details of eApeiron's invisible ink marker technology is being closely guarded, the firm's digital marker technology can be easily integrated into complex supply chains. This integration of the digital marker technology into complex supply chains results in, in effect, digital signatures being attached to multiple carriers within a logistics network.[23] As long as these carriers have digital signatures in place, the prospect of losing, misplacing or allowing replacement products into the supply chain become minimized. This digital marking of products from the producer to the distributor and finally through to the retailer ensures that any manipulation of the product is immediately identified.

Additionally, counterfeit goods either have poor imitations of the digital marking technology that do not reflect the appropriate encryption and data or do not have digital markers at all. The presence or absence of such technology on products ensures that both transportation firms and retailers are able to immediately identify counterfeit products. While in prior eras logistics firms and operators might have argued that identifying counterfeit products was not part of their formal purview, in the current era, identification of such products most certainly is part of their formal purview. Those logistics firms that do not put digital marking technology in place within the supply chain become, in essence, complicit in the new product counterfeiting industry. Saudi Arabia, as a market, seeks to not only develop its global reputation for technological advancement and financial management as a means to attract foreign investment but it also seeks to establish its reputation as an ethical marketplace where IP is protected at all levels of business and industry. Achieving such a reputation as an ethical marketplace for foreign firms depends in no small part on the use and deployment of digital marking technology. Counterfeit and fake goods in the supply chain benefits no-one except for those firms that manufacture such goods.

The advantage for Saudi Arabia and the Vision 2030 of such digital marking technology is that foreign investors can be assured that their IP and related brands are protected. It also assures them that they have the legal recourse in such markets to address counterfeit products in the supply chain when they are detected within a particular nation's supply chain facilities. Considering the long recognized difficulty in protecting IP in markets such as China, making the Jazan City For Primary and Downstream Industries and other economic cities in Saudi Arabia brand compliant ensures that the Vision 2030 itself is extremely attractive to foreign investors interested in doing business in the nation. By some accounts, 84% of all seized counterfeit products currently originate in China and Hong Kong.[24]

In fact, China provides such an effective benchmark for Jazan City for Primary and Downstream Industries and King Abdullah Economic City not because of what it has accomplished in in digital marking technology but because of its prominence as a marketplace in the counterfeit goods industry worldwide. By many estimates China overall accounts for about 89-90% of all counterfeit trade globally either directly as a producer of such goods or as a market for them or both. This has grown into such an issue for global brands because China, as does the Kingdom, has a non-English national script that dominates its own web and internet sites which makes digital identification of counterfeit goods difficult. Yet, while there are numerous online marketplaces within China which sell and market counterfeit goods directly to local consumers, the Chinese government has made significant strides in combatting counterfeit goods over the past several years. This attention given to stopping counterfeit goods producers and their transportation is also a valuable lesson that Saudi Arabia can take away from China.

This may seem like such fake and counterfeit goods are not the Kingdom's problem but what Saudi Arabia and its economic centers do not want to allow is for Jazan and King Abdullah Economic City to become what Hong Kong and China have become to global trade. That is, city leaders do not want these economic centers to become a key manufacturing center and logistics hub for counterfeit products. There are a host of different solutions and approaches to combat this issue. While the use of solutions like invisible ink that can be digitally traced is a unique application of an older technology, there are other strategies as well. Some of the current different and sometimes competing solutions are displayed in the graphic below:

Figure 15: Digital Authentication Process

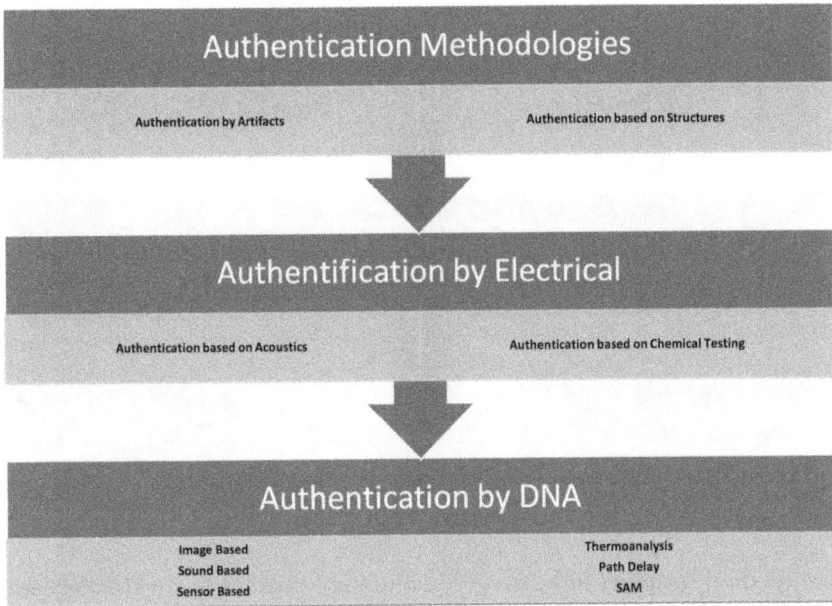

As this figure attests, digital marking as a technology can be achieved through one of several approaches. As the information points out, chemical markers on products can be read in such a manner that produces a digital signal which can then be converted to logistics data within the supply chain. Regardless of the approach, digital markers are functionally electronic scents that are attached to products within the global supply chain. Still, for the most part, digital markers are associated with some sort of digital signal producing technology such as RFID, near field communications or NFC as well as simple visual inspections at times:

Figure 16: Digital Authentication Process

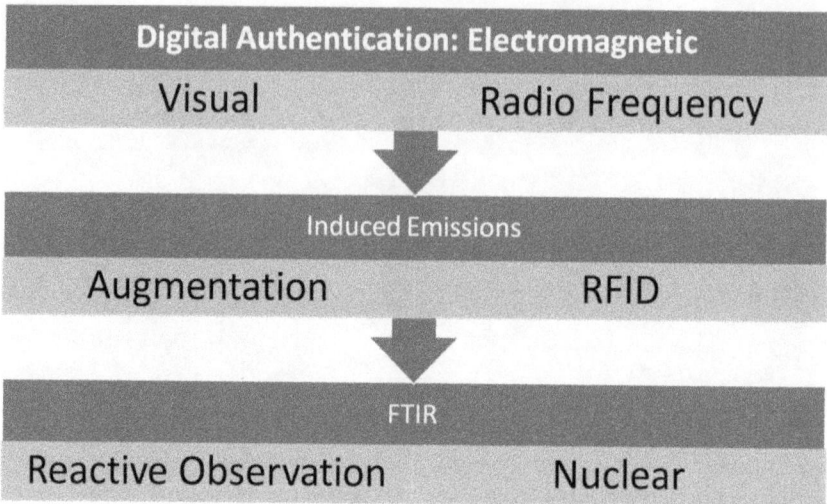

Digital Authentication: Electromagnetic	
Visual	Radio Frequency

Induced Emissions	
Augmentation	RFID

FTIR	
Reactive Observation	Nuclear

As these graphics indicate, the technology exists that can virtually detect fake and counterfeit goods. Additionally, many if not most of these different solutions can be integrated digitally into the SCM platform utilized by the logistics firm managing the supply chain.

In essence, the digital tracers produced by many of these different solutions results in visibility all along the supply chain. It also ensures that those producers, distributors and retailers who have the specialized sensors can immediately detect if a product or good is counterfeit or not. This solution is being paired with other solutions such as Blockchain also utilized by Alibaba as a means to ensure the legitimacy of products within the global supply chain. Blockchain in particular is a solution that is a comprehensive ledger or database of all online peer-to-peer transactions between vendors, suppliers, distributors, retailers and consumers in which all products associated with these transactions are assigned an ID that is both unique and traceable.[25] E-commerce platforms like Alibaba absolutely must embrace digital tracking technology because they are often the most visible virtual platform that outside participants in the logistics industry come into contact with and utilize. Clearly, the Kingdom's economic centers not only would be well-advised to adopt some form of this digital marking technology but actually must adopt some type of digital marking or digital tracing application.

Without it, international retailers and major international corporations will hesitate to invest in the Kingdom in fear of facing the same sort of IP threats to global copyrights, patents and trademarks that they have within some Asian countries. Hence, once assigned, these unique IDs travel with the assigned product up and down the entire length of the global supply chain to the final end-user or end-consumer.

This traceability within the Blockchain matrix is achieved through the attachment of a Near Field Communications chip such as an RFID chip or a QR code. The result is a traceable, visible and immutable product ID that is associated with actual real-world exchanges and transactions. This allows products within the global supply chain to travel from node to node to node with a clear transaction path visible to everyone that has access to the logistics platform or to the SCM system being utilized. Furthermore, the unique ID attached to each and every product within the global supply chain is also fully encrypted. This type of encryption means that there is both a public and a private key which ensures that authenticity of each product can be readily verified. This is because encryption ensures that a product cannot be exchanged, substituted or removed without a gap being created in the data path. If such an interruption occurs anywhere along the supply chain it is immediately visible to anyone who is able to scan the associated QR code or read the NFC tag be it RFID or other similar digital marker. Having this type of counterfeit prevention solution in place and in a manner that is integrated into existing transportation processes within Jazan and King Abdullah Economic City means that major international firms do not have to invest in such technology solutions from the ground up as it were. This results in a strong financial rationale for investment in the Kingdom as well as a strong operations and geographic market based rationale for investment.

If one is to examine or discuss the use of digital marker technologies in order to prevent the growth of counterfeit goods in Saudi Arabia, one must understand the relevance of this issue to the Vision 2030. Both Jazan and King Abdullah Economic City along with other important economic centers within the Kingdom depend on their capacity to attract foreign investment. Digital marking technology is simply one solution that can be used to enhance the Kingdom's attractiveness compared to other markets actively seeking foreign investors in the form of major international companies. Yet, digital marketing technology also ensures the Kingdom's government that it maximizes its own trade related revenues as well since excise taxes, customs fees and so forth are typically underpaid with respect to counterfeit and fake goods. Furthermore, major global brands and global firms must recognize that they are not just welcome but that their lines of business are protected from illegal activity either through intellectual property protections or through advanced operational processes. Either way, several important targets in the Vision 2030 depend directly on these factors as well: 1) shift the nation from being the 19th largest economy globally to at least the 15th largest global economy and 2) elevate the private sector's contribution to GDP from 40% to at least 65% or more.[26] Both of these key targets in the Vision 2030 are directly impacted by the successful implementation of digital marking technology as a means to reduce or prevent the growth in counterfeiting in the Kingdom. Those major international firms that recognize that the Kingdom is serious about preventing counterfeiting from turning into a cottage industry as it has in China will be much more inclined to invest in the Kingdom's economic centers and zones.

CHAPTER V
Wearable Tech, WIFI and Workers

The contemporary workspace and certainly the workspace within the context of supply chain management (SCM) has enormous opportunities to improve efficiency through wearable technology. Wearable tech includes a host of different types of technology forms from smartwatches to Fitbit types of equipment as well as basic sensors that monitor different types of information. Supply chain and logistics employees that are outfitted with such wearable technology allows their location to be tracked, productivity measured and elements monitored such as ambient temperature, humidity and light levels. All of these types of factors are incredibly pertinent to the logistics and supply chain environment. In some regard, wearable technology, networked logistics facilities and always on/always available internet access create an alternative logistics space in which the work of logistics can be re-appropriated to the benefit of product management.

For instance, many products and many types of supplies must be stored and inventoried within controlled environments. These controlled environments can be those involving temperature controlled or monitored environments, humidity controlled environments or secure and time constrained environments.[27] While these controlled environments can certainly be maintained without wearable technology, such wearable tech improves their overall efficacy and that of the supply chain that supports them. Thus, wearable tech provides a ready, off-the-shelf solution that can be easily distributed to supply chain staff as a means to achieve this type of monitoring necessary to maintain such controlled environments(see note m). Often, supply chain events that disrupt the supply chain go unnoticed for a period of time before they are identified or able to be dealt with. Wearable tech improves the ability of the supply chain operator to address such unanticipated supply chain events before they disrupt the entire supply chain. Alternatively, wearable tech can provide supply chain operators with another strategy to mitigate and minimize such disruptions when they do occur. Although sensor technology exists that can accomplish the same thing, wearable technology is fully mobile, immediately actionable and can be instantaneously processed by a worker onsite.

Basically, wearable technology provides certain attributes to contemporary firms that provide them with the actual means to sustain or to establish competitive advantage in their marketplaces. Hence, one of the most redeeming qualities of wearable technology in general within the supply chain is that it improves firm adaptability, agility and flexibility in several ways. Options within the global supply chain are always welcome compared to a lack of options when faced with difficult transportation and shipping problems. These ways in which wearable technology imparts adaptability, agility and flexibility to those firms that adopt it are discussed below:[28][29]

1. Synchronization: the digitization of information allows this information to be shared instantaneously and across all platforms which works to align all the internal processes of a firm
   a. Logistics data involved: POS data, production and inventory schedules, forecasting
2. Logistics planning: wearable technology facilitates activities such as the mapping of supply chains which results in the reduction or eradication of activities that detract value such as the amount of time in inventory of a given product
   a. Duplicated activities are removed and activities based on tradition are eradicated
3. Partnering with suppliers/vendors: partnerships can be supported in which the logistics staff in the supplier/vendor are able to provide critical product data directly to the client firm which supports business process re-engineering and the transfer of competitive intelligence/best practices/benchmarking data

4. Reductions in logistics complexity: wearable technology can result in the reduction of product variation, overly diverse bills of lading in transportation and systemic product changes while supporting greater product/order customization for the end-consumer and sub-assembly opportunities across the supply chain

5. Downstream supply chain final product configuration, assembly and distribution

6. Management of business processes: wearable tech allows business processes to be maintained in a horizontal fashion
   a. Cross-functional team building can occur across departments, divisions and business units with wearable tech

7. Collection of most effective performance related data that in turn is leveraged as a means to improve productivity within the supply chain

Thus, the benefits of wearable technology go much further than simply improving specific efficiencies within a single node of the supply chain. Rather, wearable technology supports the competitive sustainability of the firm that employs it in one respect or another. Wearable tech both increases worker productivity and effectiveness as well as improves worker accountability in the supply chain environment. Workers that do not have a wearable technology device are essentially free to do as they wish but workers who are tasked with wearable technology are not—they must conform to the demands of the technology that they are wearing.

Of all the different form factors involving wearable technology in the supply chain and logistics industry, one of the more emergent solutions in the supply chain that is currently gaining traction in the industry is that of smart glasses. After Google essentially pioneered the practicality of smart glasses as well as the functional utility of them several years ago, it is their application within the supply chain that has bolstered their wider adoption across industries. Smart glasses are currently being utilized by major transportation and delivery firms such as DHL which has integrated them into the firm's order picking and fulfilment centers. The smart glasses currently in use at DHL, referred to as the "Vision Picking" program, provide critical information and capabilities to fulfillment staff in the firm's warehouses to include: 1) instructions on each order, 2) information on item location, 3) placement of an item on a cart or vehicle and 4) verification that the right item has been manipulated.[30] The increase in both productivity and order fulfilment accuracy is remarkable. Smart glasses worn by fulfilment center staff have improved DHL's productivity in its supply chain by some 15% due to increase order accuracy, fewer item returns, reduced item loss and improved consumer satisfaction that results in increased item shipping. Additionally, one indirect benefit for DHL and other supply chain firms that utilize smart glasses is that the staff that wear them are now essentially able to free their hands for other uses as opposed to holding onto printed order sheets and so forth. This results in fewer worksite accidents, faster order picking and the aforementioned reduction in item errors.

All of these various factors can affect factors such as shelf life, product longevity and fulfillment times and so forth. Furthermore, wearable tech can improve the quality of life of the workers themselves such as monitoring heartrate, body temperature and similar feedback that can inform worksite managers when workers are experiencing higher than normal stress levels. These too can impact how efficient supply chain facilities are operated. In essence, such wearable tech is aligned with the core elements of the Vision 2030 imperatives which focus on elevating Saudi Arabia's status internationally as a global hub that supports a quality life for international firms and their employees. Overall, the inclusion of wearable tech into the global supply chain is projected to reach more than US$19 billion in value during 2018 with items such as wearable tablets surpassing more than 406 million individual units in use throughout the global supply chain.[31] These types of wearables and others are certain to populate Saudi Arabia's own supply chain operations in time. Since these technologies are, for practical intents and purposes, already mature industries in their own right, transplanting them into the supply chain and logistics operations in the Kingdom's major economic centers is not an unreasonable objective.

In this fashion, established best practices in wearable tech is already available to firms operating in the Kingdom's economic cities. Those firms that opt to improve their logistics and supply chain services as a means to attract foreign investment and economic participation in the Kingdom can merely transplant these best practices into their own warehouse, fulfillment and intermodal facilities within the Kingdom. For instance, relying on DHL's smart glasses logistics solution provides the perfect benchmark for fulfillment best practices. The image below outlines how this wearable technology solution can be easily setup and installed within the context of any logistics based operation. The best practice, as it were, details the actual hardware platform (Google Glass), the software application (VuzixM100) and also the type of supply chain activity involved (order picking and fulfillment):

Figure 17: Fulfilment Process at DHL

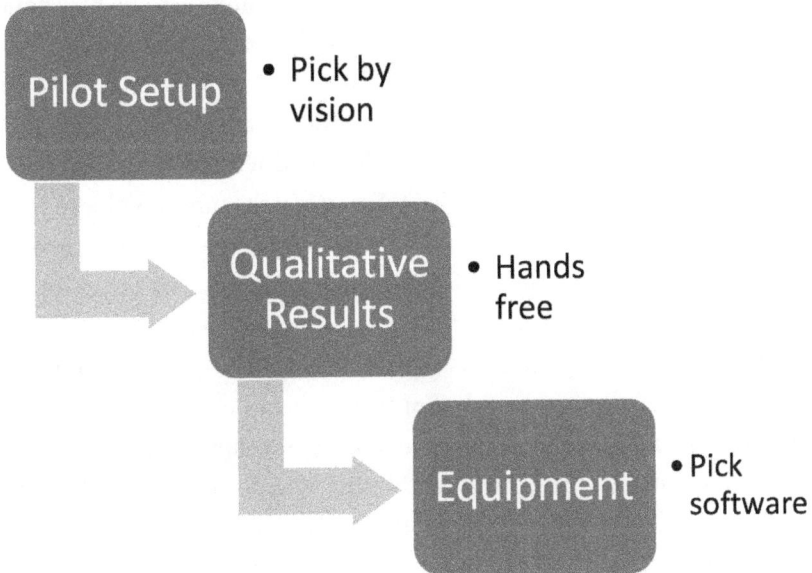

In this logistics solution, all fulfillment center staff were able to by-pass the traditional use of a handheld scanner, paper orders and manual referral back to a computer desktop or workstation. Additionally, specific gains in productivity in the fulfillment centers alone were more than 25% which eventually percolated out to the entire supply chain as a 15% gain in productivity overall. These types of productivity gains are difficult to achieve in an environment where 1 to 2% improvements are seen as strategically relevant. Also, as the graphic displays, the time per task is greatly reduced utilizing DHL's augmented reality platform centered on its smart glasses application.

Yet, smart glasses are only one element within the broader wearable tech wave that is taking over the logistics and supply chain industry. There are numerous other wearable technologies currently in development that are rapidly changing the way that SCM is conducted. Smart watches are also being integrated into the supply chain for workers that benefit from rapid access to SCM data on items, products and SKUs and so forth as well as advances made in point-of-transaction and point-of-sale activities that can now be conducted via smart watch applications. Smart watches in particular are especially beneficial within the logistics center because they excel at near field communications or NFC applications, can integrate GPS functionality and also support short range communications.[32] Another unique advantage associated with smart watch form factors is that employees are, in general, accustomed to wearing them. Employees are inundated with a host of demands in the contemporary workspace. By relying on a form factor that is familiar to most employees, this in effect works to maximize the likelihood that smart watch-based wearable technology will actually be used in a consistent fashion within the supply chain. Smart watches are now able to monitor a range of different operations of a logistics provider which empowers its logistics personnel on the worksite and in the supply chain environment.

These advantages are in addition to their ability to link up with other wearable technology platforms. The linking up of wearable technology works to expand the functionality of these devices exponentially. If such devices were capable of monitoring inventory levels by themselves, for instance, when linked with other wearable tech and devices they may be able to forecast future demand, identify bottlenecks before they occur and isolate units/items that are damaged or in distress. These other technology platforms include the logistics providers' SCM technology platform itself such as ERP and the broader internet of things as a system component. Certainly, there are other forms of mobile devices that link up with these broader SCM platforms as well but few that do so with the convenience, ease of access and familiarity as the smart watch.

Clearly, smart watches have the capacity to improve all worker productivity across the board if applied systematically and thoughtfully to an existing supply chain. This improvement occurs through a number of different modalities within supply chain operations. For example such productivity improvement occurs by providing anytime/real-time access to email, texts and calls within the communications domain of a logistics operator which all work to facilitate product fulfillment, transfer and delivery at some point within the logistics process. Likewise, logistics-based smart watch technologies provide virtual instantaneous access to system data, scanning functionality via integrated camera technologies and geo-location data within the supply chain:

Figure 18: Geo-Location Equipment

As the picture shows, a worker can access critical messages that may come in while he or she is at a remote location or can find important reference data for a given product in the field. Basically, smart watches are a functional workstation that is fully mobile within a warehouse, fulfillment or intermodal facility.

Still, both smart watches and smart glasses are evolutionary iterations of age-old technologies. The fundamental watch and the basic eyeglass is 100s of years old and offer absolutely nothing new in terms of their form factor.

It is only the application of emergent technology to these form factors that creates entirely new uses for them in the logistics and supply chain environment. While "smart" in function, the form factors that these devices rely on is essentially antiquated. Smart glasses are based on old-fashion eyewear modalities that, in and of themselves, were never ideal given the fact that they must be worn on one's face and held in place either mechanically or through design. Likewise, smart watches rely on the concept of a wrist band that must be attached to an individual's wrist in some manner and therefore is subject to work related activities such as falling off, getting hit or catching on clothing or some other type of equipment. One still developing wearable technology solution that is in the process of being integrated into both the industrial and the retail marketplace is on-skin user interface technology. This is a wearable technology that is meant to lower the intrusive nature of technology for the individual worker. This technology is being led by a company called Duoskin which was founded through technology developed at MIT that produces wearable circuitry that resembles skin art such as tattoos.

Duoskin produces wearable circuitry that can be worn in much the same manner as a tattoo by the logistics employee in the supply chain. This is a wearable circuitry that has the capacity to sense touch-based input, heat thermochromatic displays, supporting NFC with other wearables and network nodes and to simultaneously be completely inobtrusive to the user.[33] These wearable skin interfaces can be designed to operate a range of other wearables or remote operating systems on a fully mobile basis. The technology is quite remarkable in that, unlike most other wearable technologies and especially skin related wearables for workers, the Duoskin solution is relatively inexpensive to design, fabricate and introduce into a work-based environment. Research indicates that Duoskin in particular is fabricated from materials that are available from every day, commonplace sources such as craft stores and large box retailers such as temporary tattoo paper, real and imitation gold leaf along with similar materials.[34] These characteristics ensure that Duoskin and wearable circuitry in general is certain to occupy a substantial segment of the wearable technology space in the logistics industry. Hence, while this type of wearable technology is not yet fully mature, its construction, design and functionality, seen below, ensures that it will be fully applicable within the logistics and supply chain industry relatively soon:

Figure 19: Wearable Electronic Sensors

AUGMENTED REALITY

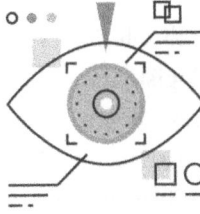

EYETAP

AR GLASSES

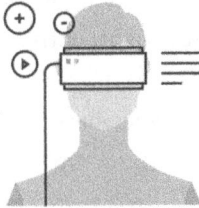

VIRTUAL REALITY

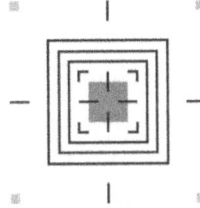

TAGS & MARKERS

TELEPRESENCE

SOFTWARE

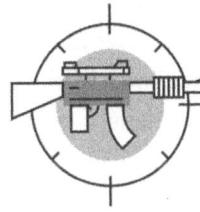

VR GAMING

TRACKING DEVICES

As the images above reveal, not only do these skin-based interfaces lack any protruding elements but they are completely unnoticeable if kept underneath clothing. The researchers that have developed DuoSkin not only have created what amount to beautiful and intriguing wearable designs that make them attractive to employees that may be tasked with wearing them but they have already designed them with the capability to operate certain smartphone applications. While their actual application and use within the logistics and supply chain field is still evolving, there are a series of established uses. These uses of the wearable circuitry include, among others, the designing of them to operate mobile scanners, recognize individual or collective item transactions and track user movements among other applications and uses.

Furthermore, wearable tech solutions such as DuoSkin are the glamorous aspect of this particular logistics trend but other more mundane solutions are actually producing more practicable and tangible applications. The supply chain and logistics industry is one that involves repetitive processes that are based on iterative results over time. That is, logistics employees are tasked with performing the same tasks over and over again such that variation in the system is almost always associated with an increase in cost factors. Therefore, technology that can improve employee productivity while simultaneously removing some of the more venal aspects of an activity benefits the entire system. One such solution that lacks DuoSkin's glamor but directly improves supply chain productivity is a novel voice-based order fulfillment solution based on a wearable headphone and microphone technology. There are several of these voice-based order fulfillment platforms in the logistics industry currently being utilized. However, one of the most successful is the Honeywell Intelligrated voice-based application. Honeywell Intelligrated offers what amounts to a 3rd party logistics solution that provides order fulfillment services to logistics operators through voice-based platforms worn at the individual worker level. Order fulfillment is one element of logistics that many retailers and suppliers are increasingly outsourcing or seeking to fully automate as a means to control or reduce costs.

This platform provides supply chain workers with a headset and a microphone such that order processors are allowed to walk or ride through a warehouse grabbing items off of shelves and placing them in containers. After each item they speak the name of the item into the microphone and then the system speaks the next item name, location and quantity into the worker's headphones allowing the worker to move on to the next order.[35] The data from this particular wearable technology application within the order fulfillment and picking process has resulted in confirmed productivity increases surpassing 15% over prior processes within logistics operations. Additionally, these productivity gains achieved more than a 99.9% order accuracy rate while simultaneously improving productivity. Productivity, order accuracy and visibility are all qualities within the global supply chain that support cost reductions along the supply chain. These types of results ensure that there is a firm's rationale for logistics and supply chain related decisions to implement wearable technology as a means to improve their operational efficiencies can be made more effectively. It is this rationale that makes wearable technology and particularly functional solutions such as Honeywell Intelligrated's voice operated wearable applications so applicable for the Kingdom's economic centers.

The Kingdom's economic cities are being developed not only within the context of the Vision 2030 but also with respect to certain economic objectives involving economic development in general. In most instances these objectives are actually shared between the Vision 2030 and the purpose of economic cities which are those including: 1) the achievement of economic diversity, 2) providing pilot models for economic development, 3) establishing regional economic growth, 4) creating jobs for local nationals, 5) attracting foreign direct investment in the Kingdom, and 6) enhancing lifestyle options for the population.[36] Clearly, while some of the wearable technology in the supply chain and logistics industries may be still too immature to achieve tangible productive results in practice, there are others that are having an immediate impact on productivity in the supply chain. These involve the aforementioned applications such as smart watches armed with sensor technology, mobile readers and similar sensors/mobile platforms that improve the functional use of the employ at various points within a logistics facility that would otherwise not be a productive location. These particular wearable tech solutions fit neatly within the Kingdom's Vision 2030 objectives as well as within its overarching purpose in establishing economic cities in the first place. The Vision 2030 has as its core objective ive the intention to ensure that the Kingdom's economy not only becomes diversified but also internationally competitive not just in the near future but into the foreseeable future. Such is the long-term vison of the Crown Prince and his innovative approach to the marketplace.

Finally, it should be noted that automation across the entire supply chain and throughout the logistics field in general will continue to change the character of the industry. The logistics field is primarily one which has embraced emerging technology as a means to improve overall performance in the industry from an operational perspective. It is one thing to implement automation and to fully automate processes but another to do so in a way that accounts for human factors. Human employees must act on the data and information generated by IT solutions in the supply chain in order for much of this data and information to be functionally useful. It is this overall level of pervasive influence on how people manage data and information that is expected to increase in percentage over the next 20 to 30 years as technological innovation continues apace (See Appendix 1 in the Appendices Section of this book). While there is some debate on the relevance of human factors in the supply chain, the interaction between people and technology is of critical importance within the logistics industry as a whole. This is especially apparent considering the ongoing expansion of wearable technology in the logistics industry.

CHAPTER VI
New Uses for Old Postal

For many years the traditional postal services offered and supported by national governments the world over were suffering as many shippers moved to private carriers and consumers shifted to digital mail. However, recently these traditional postal services are experiencing a resurgence as e-tailers and supply chain operators are recognizing the value in their well-established delivery processes. Within the concept of old postal services, the focus of the conversation is on national postal carriers such as the United States Postal Service (USPS) and similar traditional postal carriers maintained by national governments. Yet, there are other established carriers like UPS, Fedex and DHL among others that fit within this traditional delivery route model.

This is why, as part of this conversation on old and traditional postal carriers, major private carriers such as the aforementioned UPS, Fedex and DHL for example must be included to some extent in the conversation on how traditional transportation firms can be integrated most effectively into some element of a firm's overall supply chain. This is because these firms are also well-established traditional package carriers as well with a high degree of inherent granularity. Regardless then of which particular traditional carrier is utilized, the idea is that these traditional carriers such as the USPS for example, excel at delivering the product directly to the end-consumer be it a business or a retail consumer:

Figure 20: Traditional Postal Process

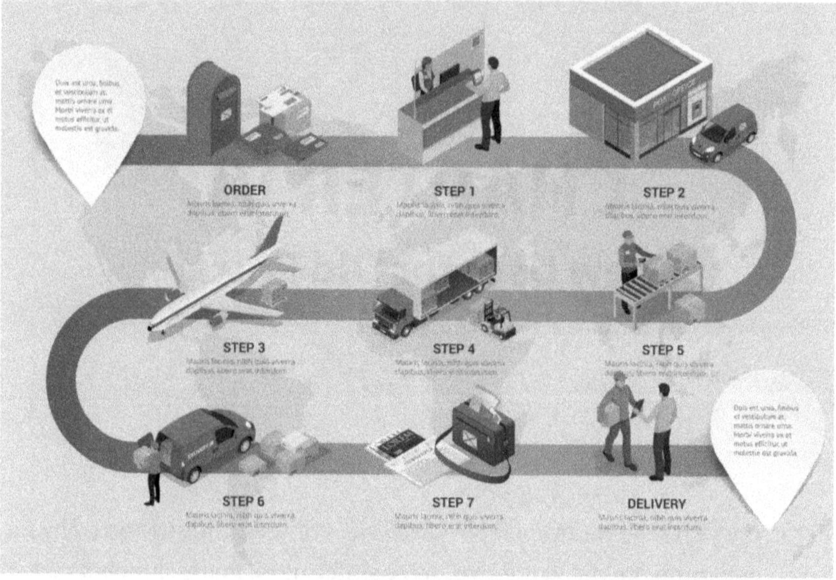

These traditional carriers already have pre-existing delivery routes in place that allow their own operations to be grafted onto a retailer's or a distributor's own supply chain. In effect, what these traditional carriers have that other 3rd party logistics providers do not have is what is referred to as route density.[37] Route density is a quality that refers to the amount of established delivery modalities, channels and pathways that are extant in any given locality. Clearly, attempting to match the route density of a postal carrier is virtually impossible considering the amount of pre-existing infrastructure that such national postal services have in place. This same feature applies to the private carriers like UPS, Fedex and DHL for instance but they are not quite as granular as national postal carriers.

Hence, within the logistics field, one critical area that e-tailers and supply chain operators are finding value in traditional postal carriers is the mechanism by which the end-consumer actually receives the product. This mechanism within the supply chain is what is referred to as "the last mile" in the supply chain. This refers to the final delivery portion of a product's transportation from the transporter or retailer to the actual end-user or end-consumer which is typically a residence or a place of business. Much of the supply chain still depends, as it were, on the simple structure of the organizations involved. As the image below accurately summarizes it, all manner of products are essentially funneled into the framework of these traditional package carriers who affect the last mile delivery requirements of a huge diversity of supply chains on a global basis:

Figure 21: Last Mile Logistics

Without the inclusion of traditional postal carriers such as the USPS, UPS and Fedex among others, logistics operators would be forced to adopt extreme measures. These extreme measures would be those like either building-out their own fixed transportation networks or simply delivering products to a central staging area and leave it up to the end-consumer, be it a retailer or consumer, to make their own arrangements for final pick-up or delivery.

For its part, the Kingdom too maintains a national postal service that has developed its own integrated delivery network. Saudi Post receives the financial and policy support of the national government and as such is well-positioned to enhance the supply chain networks of those firms that invest in the Kingdom's economic cities like Jazan. Saudi Post has already invested heavily in adapting to the global marketplace and developing a digital infrastructure for 21st century firms and their virtual SCM processes. This is evident in Saudi Post's development of its own E-Mall platform that distributors, suppliers and retailers can integrate readily into their supply chains which is accompanied by the range of traditional parcel services such as registered, express and official mail/package delivery services.[38] Since this national postal carrier's services and operations is integrated into Jazan and the other economic cities already, Saudi Post stations are critical to effective logistics operations. Saudi Post has not only an existing transportation and fulfillment infrastructure but are also placed at strategic facilities within the Kingdom's economic centers which only enhances the cities' attraction to outside investors.

Basically, Saudi Post as well as the major international carriers, provide the fundamental matrix through which the Kingdom's economic cities are integrated into the global trade framework. That is, the supply chain and the logistics industry in general still must navigate the global marketplace within the constraints of how the different entities that make up the supply chain are arranged. Within the supply chain, there is often a tendency for each entity to create separate functions in order to seek the optimization of their own performance outcomes. The result is often the development of certain logistics phenomena such as inventory buffers, bottlenecks perhaps and also time lags in the various interfaces that exist between logistics entities as well as logistics units within single entities. In order to overcome these types of issues, the supply chain needs to be or should be arranged in such a way as to act as a single synchronized network. Such a complex network requires a higher level of process alignment across the supply chain. This complex network is one which itself benefits from a much greater level of collaborative exchanges. By co-opting, in some sense, the existing competencies of established organizations like the postal service that exists in most markets, such collaborate exchanges can be facilitated with minimal cost to the logistics agency or agencies involved.

Thus, within this type of synchronization imperative the logistic requirement for achieving maximum efficiencies at minimal costs can be met. This requirement is that in which product shipments can be made more frequently, more reliably and more efficiently according to consumer criteria than they could otherwise be met by the logistics firm acting alone. In fact, the established delivery channels and the inherent preexisting granularity related to traditional postal services causes these established carriers to even partner with each other. Fedex and the USPS for instance have an operating agreement for certain classifications of delivery for air transportation. In this operating agreement the national postal service, USPS, actually contracts with Fedex to deliver its own priority and express mail packages via Fedex's in-house airline system.[39] In this regard, the USPS still leverages its route density for on-ground deliveries but relies on Fedex's fixed, high-speed supply chain channel (its own airline) as a means to connect the local and regional nodes of the supply chain. This solution is very consumer oriented because the USPS' only other options are to: a) maintain its own airline (very expensive and resource dependent) or b) rely on the national airlines and their established flight paths (expensive and unreliable). Thus, traditional carriers resolve supply chain problems not only for suppliers, vendors, producers, distributors and retailers but for each other as well.

Through this active seeking out of economies of scale, partnerships are critical. Partnerships work to improve efficiencies through the development of supply chain partners such as the postal service and this, in turn, results in the ability of consumers or client firms own ability to ship more products. This is because they become discouraged from the ordering of smaller quantities which essentially end up costing the same or similar to ship as do larger quantities because of the volume quotient. This outcome achieved through partnering with national postal carriers occurs because of the logistics price penalties and base product delivery schedules of the postal service involving small orders, batches or shipments. Transportation carriers experience these types of penalties as they attempt to optimize the efficiency of their routes in which some routes may be discontinued due to low volume orders which makes them cost-inefficient.

It also occurs because the postal service typically excels at achieving a higher level of consolidation of items and item deliveries. Thus, partnering with established postal carriers presents an attractive opportunity to logistics management. This opportunity relates to finding ways in which these postal carrier features can be achieved without resulting in escalation of shipment costs for the end-consumer but in a way that lowers the costs of transportation for the logistics provider. Much of this competitive advantage in partnering with existing postal carriers can be achieved by:

1. Identifying shipment, replenishment and inventorying requirements further up the supply chain and even the commodity chain
2. Executing a higher level of forecasting discipline
3. Combining product orders from multiple suppliers/vendors into a
   single delivery schedule and modality
4. Utilization of cross-docking opportunities with the postal service

The entire character of the global supply chain is changing towards an idea in which the supply chain and all of the firms involved in it is essentially what amounts to an extended enterprise. Therefore, 3rd party logistics and particularly the integration of traditional postal carriers removes functional barriers to last mile deliveries. The result is a much more horizontal supply chain management process that removes the traditional separation between vendors, suppliers, distributors, consumers and logistics providers.

Traditional postal carriers have the established granularity in virtually every community that supply chain operators do not. Such supply chain operators simply cannot build-out these types of dense delivery routes in a meaningful way. Additionally, traditional postal carriers also maintain the product volume within their own established supply chains to take advantage of economies of scale throughout their entire supply chain environment. In essence, supply chain and logistics firms can basically piggy back on many of a traditional postal carrier's services while adding value through their own unique logistics services. One way that the Jazan City For Primary And Downstream Industries and other economic centers within Saudi Arabia can improve their own logistics and supply chain services is to develop partnerships with many of these traditional postal carriers in the major economic markets from which their largest investors originate from. This allows many of these international investors in the Jazan City For Primary And Downstream Industries and other economic zones to control costs.

In this regard, it should be noted that Saudi Post has developed an in-house parcel delivery service that is directly linked to the goals and objectives of the Vision 2030. By linking this in-house parcel delivery service directly to the Vision 2030, the Saudi government led by Crown Prince Mohammed creates an informal mandate that all commercial enterprises in the Kingdom should act on a policy of economic diversification. This in-house parcel service is identified as EMS or Express Mail Service whose mission and vision is to respond to local and international clients and their needs for "express mail and parcels operator in the Kingdom and also become among the best providers of the service internationally."[40] Hence, EMS is a platform within the Kingdom's national postal service that was erected specifically to affect the Vision 2030's edicts for international diversification of its business environment.

The logistics and supply chain industry primarily involves the management and oversight of a transportation network of some kind. Virtually all manner of companies among most industries utilize or require some form of supply chain and distribution chain. These supply and distribution chains are either managed in-house by these companies or are contracted out in some respect to 3rd party providers such as UPS, Fedex, and DHL, for example. A supply chain is typically described as being the total of all retail distribution outlets, distribution points, transportation methods and routes, product inventories and production facilities, as well as suppliers, vendors and other related transportation nodes.[41] The supply chain is a critical aspect of any company's operations and competitive profile. A supply and distribution network that is poorly managed and that subsequently suffers from phenomena such as bottlenecks or excess product inventory levels, among other issues, can undermine profitability. Thus, firms shipping products either immediately or eventually experience losses in revenue and customers or clients.

Some of the most recognized 3rd party supply chain providers are of course UPS, FedEx, and DHL among others. These companies might be thought of by some as parcel delivery companies but, in fact, supply chain management is a significant part of their businesses. These companies form deep and meaningful relationships with the companies that they contract with to provide 3rd party logistics services. Researchers in the field have demonstrated that these 3rd party logistics providers in the transportation and logistics industry are successful because they often develop revenue models that are integrated across each of their enterprise platforms.[42] The outcome of these types of shared revenue structures among 3rd party logistics providers and the companies that they serve is such that a greater degree of innovation is achieved. This then improves the supply chain efficiencies between both the vendor-manufacturer relationship and the manufacturer-distributor relationship. Essentially, companies such as UPS and FedEx have invested resources in the successful outcome of their clients' businesses and this mutually beneficial approach to logistics operations benefits both types of enterprises.

Perhaps the most recognized transportation and logistics related firm in the world is UPS. UPS is well-known for its parcel delivery services but also maintains other logistics services such as freight forwarding, truckload and less than a truckload cargo transportation services, as well as supply chain operations and management for clients.[43] The company maintains several main divisions within its operations which are its North American Domestic Parcel Operations, International Parcel Operations, and the company's Supply Chain & Freight Operations which scale from small businesses to large multi-nationals. UPS has established operations across more than 175 countries and is expanding rapidly across China which it views as its primary growth market.

DHL is one of UPS' and FedEx' most significant international competitors. Despite the firm's international presence, its North American market presence has been substantially reduced over the past decade or so. DHL established itself as the go-to shipping company for many 3rd world markets in which the larger carriers like UPS and Fedex along with national postal services either did not exist or operated only marginally. It is clear that the global economic framework has affected DHL as well as the broader logistics industry but the firm is still a recognized logistics service provider. The company divides its operations into a series of core activities such as parcel delivery and logistics services. The company's logistics services involve air, ocean, and rail freight operations as well as back-office supply chain solutions to manage these operations.[44] While the company's North American business has suffered it is still one of the most recognized international logistics industry brands. Likewise, FedEx is also one of the more visible transportation and logistics providers in the world. The company has established itself as strong performer in the overall logistics industry. Fedex is a major revenue producer in the logistics industry but its business is high cost as well because of its large fleet of aircraft and transportation infrastructure. FedEx' operating divisions consist of its FedEx Express, FedEx Ground, FedEx Freight, and FedEx Services in which the company is able to develop seamless logistics solutions for its clients.

The use of established shipping companies such as Fedex, UPS and of course, national postal carriers affects the supply chain in different ways. These positive effects are such that they can be characterized through three individual qualities. These three individual performance qualities are: 1) efficiencies achieved through partnerships, 2) organizational and supply chain effectiveness and 3) adaptability of the logistics process in general (See Appendix 2 in the Appendices section of this text). There are times, according to this rationale, that partnering with established organizations is much more cost-effective and even operationally effective than attempting to recreate similar systems in-house. Additionally, any time that a logistics operator attempts to develop new services, supply chain extensions or similar outcomes independently, this creates a resource drag that is difficult to account for both financially and operationally. Simply put, incorporating these traditional carriers into the supply chain offers logistics operators the opportunity to improve performance outcomes such as cost sharing and reduction, supply chain responsiveness and even the improvement of relationships with suppliers, vendors and clients.

The supply chain within the logistics industry in which the postal service is a key segment adopts a unique marketing perspective. The postal carrier within the broader logistics industry in general is a mix of both products and services evidenced by the postal carrier's typical operations. These are operations in which both shipper accommodations and customer services have to be supplied at the same time. Consequently, the supply chain within this products-services orientation in the logistics industry involves a series of key elements from a purely logistics perspective:[45]

1. Supply chain agility which is necessary to ensure that product inventory levels are maintained adequately in order to ensure supply on an ad-hoc basis determined by shipper/consumer demand

2. Logistics capacity in which product/item shipments must be coordinated in sufficient supply while adequate levels of supporting material shipping containers, packing material and so forth must be maintained

3. Shipper/consumer satisfaction utilized as a measure of overall supply chain performance is already implemented

4. Pricing stability such that shipment accommodation, container and shipping costs do not fluctuate to broadly within the marketplace

5. Information where counter personnel, shipper/consumer services and postal carrier equipment maintenance all have access to shipper/consumer data, service history and transportation requirements

All of these elements affect both the efficiency of the postal carrier supply chain as well as the marketing message that the postal carrier is able to utilize.

The integration of the traditional postal carrier into the global supply chain can be partially facilitated through the use of established technologies in the marketplace. These established technologies are those including RFID technology which is discussed in an earlier chapter. Much of the support for RFID solutions in the postal service involves its relationship to the generation of shipment data and data tracking. Supply chain factors such as visibility, transparency and order accuracy depend upon the effective and efficient production of usable data. RFID is specifically a technology that is capable of both generating and also of capturing data without any form of manual intervention on the part of the postal carrier or its staff. In fact, the USPS is actively soliciting bid proposals for some type of NFC solution for mail tracking in general in which RFID, blue tooth or other wireless communication protocol is integrated into its own logistics system as a means to track mail.[46] These NFC based technologies within the traditional postal services facilitates complete package/product transparency and visibility up and down the supply chain. The result is such that consumers can virtually locate their product anywhere within the supply chain. This is accomplished by the marriage of on-site, NFC based sensors that feed data into the USPS' technology infrastructure that all USPS sites access. In turn, this package and mail data then populates the USPS' various databases, servers and systems that its consumer facing web-based platform accesses. This then allows consumers to input their item data and the system locates the item relative to its physical location at the time of the consumer inquiry:

Figure 22: Postal Service Tracking

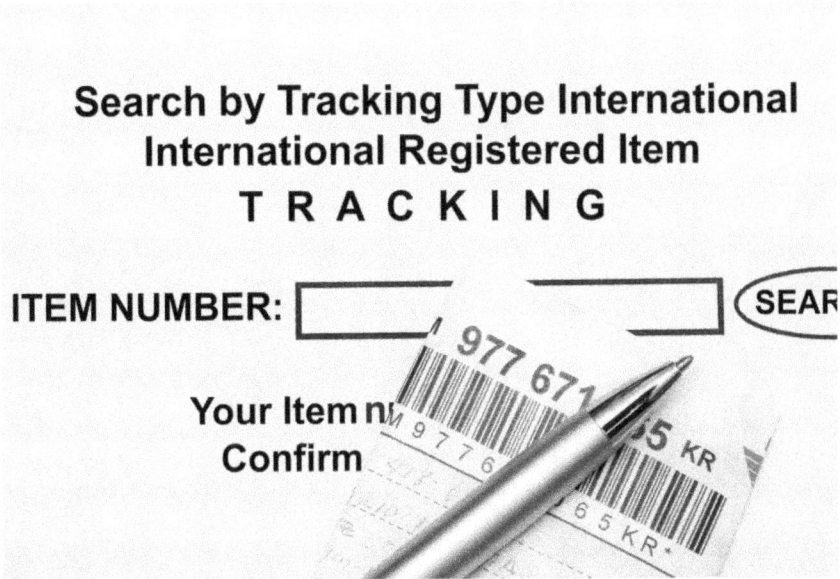

While not fully mature, this type of supply chain tracking and visibility feature is certain be developed within the next few years.

In turn, the cost-benefits and competitive advantages of integrating traditional carriers into a supply chain will only continue to expand for 3rd party logistics providers, retailers and others who have to build, maintain and support a supply chain network. This in turn supports the creation of supporting control systems with automated responses as well as real-time inventory tracking and fulfillment operations of the postal carrier itself.[47] All of these operations are inherently data dependent such that a failure of the on-ground sensors results in a failure of the on-line services provided by the system. This is why robust, encrypted and secure technology platforms are vital for logistics providers. All of these different attributes related to RFID use and deployment improve the efficiency of any commercial operations and this certainly applies to the logistics industry as it does to any other.

CHAPTER VII
Standards and Sustainability

Many nations and the commercial enterprises that operate in them are now focused on factors such as sustainability and carbon footprints. These elements are all part of what is referred to as their corporate social responsibility or CSR policies and platforms. As an important aspect of firm operations then, the supply chain is, increasingly, a central player in these firms' CSR objectives. This is because, for many firms, the majority of their carbon emissions as well as their overall energy usage originates within the context of their supply chains which are, by definition, transportation and delivery oriented. For example, a firm's logistics operations and supply chain never completely shuts down. Important activities such as warehousing, storage and fulfillment centers often operate on a 24/7 basis. All of these various activities within the supply chain includes electrical consumption to operate equipment and lights, facilities operations to include heating and air conditioning and a host of other cost producing and energy using operations.

Suturing all of these logistics nodes together is the actual transportation network itself. This logistics network consists of trucks hauling goods and supplies, trains moving goods and supplies and ships moving goods and supplies. This consumes an enormous amount of fuel, produces an enormous amount of greenhouse gases in the form of emissions and adds considerable cost to the supply chain. The supply chain, in one form or another, creates massive corporate social responsibility (CSR) issues for firms up and down the supply chain. This applies to both supply chain operators as well as the client firms that depend on them. One solution to these issues that is currently being developed is the use of standards that provide a framework from which supply chain firms can develop strategies to reduce emissions, energy use and improve efficiency.

Logistics standards and guidelines are a kind of actionable expression of supply chain theory put into practice. The development of standards in the logistics field requires the application of value analysis within supply chain science. Value analysis refers to the act of consciously analyzing various logistics related components, activities and shared processes within the typical supply chain. The objective ive within value analysis as a logistics theory is to assign what amounts to a quantifiable value to each individual process or activity within the supply chain.[48] The focus is on the identification of those specific logistic processes or activities that are not necessarily contributing value to the logistics function of any given logistics operator. Value analysis is a theory and practice that implements a series of factors that are each quantified in some way. The focus is on being able to arrive at a true and accurate cost-benefit of every logistics related activity across the entire supply chain. This series of factors consists of those that include actual cost, the unique functionality of the task or objective, and even the long-term utility of the product or service that is being delivered to the end-consumer or end-user.[49] This overall analytical process is extremely rigorous in character. It forces each logistics operator to ensure that all tasks and processes are subject to review. The end result is that any logistics related activities, tasks or processes that are ultimately found o add little or no value to the logistic firm's supply chain are eradicated.

The development and inclusion of standards within the supply chain also has the added benefit of reducing supply chain complexity. While some degree of complexity may be the natural result of technical integration within the supply chain, too much complexity in the supply chain inevitably creates its own set of unique issues that interfere with efficiency. The nature of the supply chain is that it benefits from iterative processes that are both time and cost efficient and that can be recreated over and over again with little to no variation within the system. Thus, identifying where complexity in the supply chain can originate allows standards and guidelines to be developed that can directly decrease or reduce such complexity from developing in the first place. Some of the more common sources of supply chain complexity then are found in the following areas:[50]

1. **Network/node complexity of the supply chain**
   o Number of supply chain nodes and links in the overall network such as those that develop from outsourcing, offshoring, 3rd party services, etc...
   o Increased likelihood for unanticipated disruptions

2. **Process/procedural complexity**
   o Internal and external complexities slowing activities down
     ▪ The production of different items on different days and so forth
   o Inclusion of long processes that have multiple activities creates extended product lead times and are also more prone to outcome variability and supply disruptions
   o Constant business process review for structural changes and adjustments in order to reengineer for efficiency

3. **Product-mix complexity**
   o A range of products and/or services often increases over time within the supply chain
   o Product/service variations increase the resource demand per each variation which adversely affects logistics activities such as inventory buffers, forecasting and component/supply ordering

4. **Product complexity**
   o Design choices affect materials required to product and ship products and their component parts
     ▪ Increasing the number of components or supplies necessary per product results in reduced product commonality, material replenishment lead times, the overall time-to-market and product order volume, supply chain volatility, and downstream issues such as post-sales support or point-of-sale customization

5. **Consumer/client complexity**
   o Presence of non-standard service options or ever-increasing customization options
   o Somewhat limited recognition of value added costs such as customization which all affect supply chain complexity

6. **Supplier/vendor complexity**
   o The overall size of the supplier and vendor base

7. **Organizational complexity**
   - ○ Industry verticality or horizontal structuring affects supply chain complexity
   - ○ Industry growth which occurs organically results in different supply chain requirements versus external means of growth such as mergers and acquisitions
8. **Information and data complexity**
   - ○ Overall volume and diversity of data
   - ○ The visibility of supply and demand

Understanding where these sources of complexity in the supply chain originate allows logistics firms to develop the mechanisms to address them. At times, complexity may be a necessity but it should always be tempered with standards that allow such complexity in the supply chain to be mediated efficiently by the supply chain participants.

Another conceptual approach to the creation and design of standards and guidelines is value engineering within the supply chain. This activity is similar in concept and even application to the practice value analysis theory. Value engineering theory is an activity that involves a systemic and organized methodology in which the unique value of a product or perhaps even the design of a logistics facility, or even an entire product or service line is examined for areas of improvement.[51] Value engineering is a formula that views the supply chain and logistics activities within a logistics operator with the mindset that the logistic system's processes can be improved or perhaps reduced in cost or maybe even both outcomes. Value engineering theory as a logistics related analytical process consists of a series of staged activity phases. These staged activity phases in value engineering are typically listed as being an information phase, an accompanying speculative phase, and then the analytical phase followed by a proposal phase.[52] One interesting characteristic of value engineering and this type of phased process is that it is designed to be implemented within a logistics team environment. This is because all logistics and supply chain functions within the supply chain are subject to examination.

The deep influence that standards, policies and guidelines can have on the supply chain is evident in the operations that Walmart maintains worldwide as part of its global supply chain. The firm is recognized as basing at least part of its sustainable competitive advantage on the efficiency of its global supply chain and it recently issued a set of standards that all of its suppliers and vendors are required to follow which include: 1) adhere to a 2-day shipping window for all products and items and 2) achieve a compliance rate of 95% as opposed to the previous 90% standard.[53] It is evident that standards, policies and guidelines issued by a logistics firm can have a pervasive impact on the supply chain and how logistics are managed both down and upstream. Even from a sustainability perspective, such standards and policies can alter the way in which the supply chain develops. For Saudi Arabia and its economic cities, even its domestic postal carrier has well-developed standards and policies. These standards and policies are such that they provide functional guidelines for logistics operators in order to integrate with the Kingdom's EMS services:[54]

Figure 23: Postal/Carrier Standards

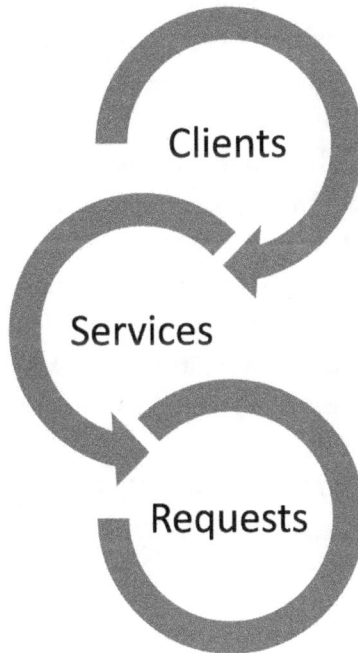

Clients

Services

Requests

In order to integrate the Kingdom's postal carrier services into Jazan City for Primary and Downstream Industries' and the other economic cities' supply chains, logistics providers merely have to access its process guidelines. Such standards and guidelines involve APIs which are application templates in a sense for integrating with the postal service's technology platform. These process guidelines provided by Saudi Post are available online and can be supported easily through established corporate IT functions and services such as API development.

All of these outcomes go on to affect in a positive way, how firms are seen publicly. This is a concern for all major international firms and is one reason that the Vision 2030 excels at attracting such FDI. For instance, one potential standard is to identify how a firm's carbon footprint is to be determined and then establish a baseline figure from which each logistics operator can develop reduction performance targets. These types of standards are being developed by organizations such as Carbon Trust and CEMARS which work to develop universal standards that each firm within each industry can apply to their operations. By adopting the most recent universal standards within the supply chain environment, the Jazan City For Primary And Downstream Industries and similar economic cities in Saudi Arabia can augment their own quality of life initiatives. Furthermore, economic city leadership can work to offer foreign investors the capacity to bolster their CSR portfolios internationally.

In terms of the actual selection and application of standards based solutions within supply chain and logistics operations, the industry has begun to formulate several key standards. These key standards are basically designed to maximize the likelihood that various supply chain solutions within logistics operations will be successful and that success is ultimately measured by 3rd party satisfaction in the form of satisfied clients or consumers. The table below works to summarize these logistics industry supply chain standards:[55]

Table 4: Supply Chain Standards and Characteristics

Supply Chain Standards	Standard Description
Maximize Supply Chain Capital Investment	* Supply chain solutions must be able to forward integrate future technologies within the logistics field * Supply Chain solutions should bring back-office as well as front-office operations together (e.g. Warehousing with Sales)

Supply Chain Standards	Standard Description
Implement Change in Supporting Logistics Processes	* Supply Chain solutions should be championed by a logistics firm's top management * Supply chain solutions should result in improved data visibility * Logistics technology platforms must be able to handle this increased amount of data, data tracking & data visibility up and down the supply chain
Simplify all Logistics Applications	* Pre-testing ensures that supply chain solutions are easy to use & easy to apply
Issues Relating to Data Security Must be Addressed	* Logistics data must be encrypted * The supply chain application must be invisible to the consumer
Logistics Efficiency Requires All Human Factors to be Considered	* Supply Chain solutions should not replace personal interaction in the constellation of the end-user experience * Supply chain solutions are not a substitute for effective logistics management

(Hozak, 2012)

These types of standards based principles and practices vis-a-vis the supply chain provides important managerial guidance for logistics professionals. Standards and guidelines, in and of themselves, are not a substitute for good logistics operations but instead enhance already good supply chain metrics. Alternatively, if poorly developed and adopted up and down the supply chain, they could also affectively worsen already poor logistics related metrics.

The analytical tools described within value analysis and value engineering are often used as interchangeable methods. However, value analysis is a logistics technique often utilized to locate specific nodes in the supply chain or related intermodal stations that are not providing value to the logistics operator.[56] Thus, such operations would somewhat limited in scope where the process of value engineering is applied not only to the supply chain but also to other related areas such as product design and development processes as well. Yet, both value analysis and the process of value engineering retain their focus on the improvement of processes within the logistic operator's operations. These operations inevitably apply to the supply chain, logistics activities and product/service related activities. One example of value analysis and value engineering being utilized in practice is when logistics analysts develop cost models of total product life-cycle costs compared to product direct costs.[57] In the case of the first example, logistics analysts determine what the costs that the logistics firm may incur over the entire life-cycle of a product or service might be. This can include such disparate costs like product marketing, product inventory and storage and even product returns. In contrast, the direct costs related to a product or service include only those costs that contribute to its actual production and distribution. These relate to costs like component, material and even transportation costs such as fuel.

In terms of practice, there are myriad examples of logistics standards being put in place within the logistics industry. One of the most visible logistics related standards currently in use throughout the global supply chain is the GS1 set of supply chain standards. These GS1 standards target transportation and logistics firms with a framework that provides them with a set of shared rules that are universally applied across the global supply chain. Typically, the GS1 supply chain standards are divided into three broad categorical forms which include master data, transactional related data and finally actual event data:

Table 5: GS1 Standards

Master Data	Transactional Data	Event Data
GDSN Connects trading partners to the global registry database	eCom Provides operating guidelines for electronic data interchange	EPCIS Standard for immediate sharing of information

Master Data	Transactional Data	Event Data
GTIN, GLN, brand owner identification, product descriptions, GPC codes, target market	GTIN GLM, SSCC, GSIN, GDTI, GRAI, purchase orders, dispatch advice, transportation instructions	What, when, where, why: SGTIN, GLN, SSCC, GIAI, GRAI, GSRN, GDTI

Without anyone of these categorical divisions of data, the global supply chain would not be able to support the level of international trade that is currently being supported. Technology platforms, regardless of vendor, all rely on these datasets in order to function reliably and to support critical logistics activities such as forecasting, inventory buffering and reordering and so on. These GS1 standards include the following:[58]

1. GS1 Identification Keys: These identification keys are a standardized taxonomy for how items, units or products are referred to and identified within the context of a supply chain
    a. Global Trade Item Number or GTIN: Every item or product is assigned its own unique identifying number
    b. Global Location Number or GLN: A unique number that is associated with places, nodes and locations within a supply chain
    c. Serial Shipping Container Code: This is a number assigned to a load or shipment which can be a case, pallet, truckload or shipload
    d. Global Returnable Asset Identifier or GRAI: This number is assigned to logistics equipment such as containers, cates, reusable pallets, containers and similar types of reusable and recyclable equipment
    e. Global Individual Asset Identifier or GIAI: Every facility, equipment asset and similar is given this number as a means for the logistics firm to catalogue its resources
    f. Global Shipment Identification Number or GSIN: Every shipper assigns this number to a unique shipment that is assembled

together under one order, one bill of lading or under a single consignee as the case may be

g. Global Identification Number for Consignment or GINC: This figure is assigned to goods or units that are assigned to a particular freight forwarding agency or individual carrier

2. GS1 Data Carriers: This series of identification keys are used to denote which particular form of media contains logistics data on any given goods, products or items in transit

a. GS1 BarCodes: These are barcodes that are encoded with all of the previously relevant codes as well as certain application identifiers which allows other data readers to detect what type of media is being read

b. EPC/RFID Tags: These are near-field communication or NFC tags using RFID technology and other forms of NFC technologies to transmit and read the GS1 Electronic Product Code data associated with any item, unit or shipment

3. GS1 Communication Standards: Communication standards ensure that the different entities that operate throughout a supply chain all adhere to the same set of communication systems

a. GS1 eCom: This system utilizes other GS1 taxonomy within the framework of electronic data exchanges that are based on universal data formats including those such as EANCOM and XML

b. GS1 Global Data Synchronisation Network or GDSN: This network relies on GS1's Global Registry format and secure site authentication as a means to ensure that supply chain operators all use the same format for information exchange

As these standards indicate, any logistics operator that is intent on joining the global supply chain in any respect can simply ascribe to these existing standards. Such standards develop and support the concept of universality with the result being that products, items and supplies are moved much more efficiently up and down the supply chain. These logistics standards in particular tend to overlay the global supply chain in the following manner:

Table 6: Universal Logistics Standards

GLN, GTIN, SSCC, GRAI, GTIN	GLN, GRAI, SSCC	GIAI, GTIN, SSCC, GLN, GSRN
Company & Location: Global Location Number (GLN)	Logistics & Shipping: Serial Shipping Container Code (SSCC), Global Identification Number for Consignment (GINC)	Assets: Global Individual Asset Identifier (GIAI), Global Returnable Asset Identifier (GRAI)
Product: Global Trade Item Number (GTIN)		Services & More: Global Service Relation Number (GSRN), Global Document Type Identifier (GDTI)

As the image depicts, each stage, leg and node within the global supply chain tends to be governed by one of these universal standards. This allows each supply chain operator to ensure that product moved along individual supply chains can be continuously tracked, monitored and managed as it shifts from one service provider to another.

Standards and guidelines are more than esoteric devices used by managers in the logistics industry to keep departments and employees in line. Rather, standards and guidelines provide the parameters in which a logistic firm's resources can be allocated methodically and in a way that accounts for environmental, organizational and human capital factors. The structure that this standards and guidelines paradigm takes within the logistics industry is seen in Appendix 3 in the Appendices section of this book. The paradigm indicates that those logistics firms that make ample use of standards and guidelines are forced to appropriately inventory their own internal resources and to assess how organizational factors such as internal knowledge, technology and finances result in technical innovation within the industry itself. It is apparent then that standards and guidelines act as a functional translation of strategy into action.

The use of standards and guidelines within the supply chain can be achieved through established approaches. Standards within the context of the supply chain are often referred to as the mechanism through which quality within logistics is achieved. Standards, policies and guidelines offer the supply chain a great deal of credibility. The reason for this is that outside reviewers of a supply chain can be certain that the data and information contained within a given logistics platform is credible, reliable and accurate. Validity of supply chain data can be established through a process identified as construct validity in which data standards and policies must reflect the following features or elements:[59]

1. The integration of multiple types and sources of data and information: supply chain and logistics operations must rely on both the existing secondary data within the supply chain as well as the information gleaned from real-time activities
2. The use and integration of a clear chain of established logistics data: logistics data must lead to the establishment of core assumptions by logistics managers which are subsequently affirmed or denied within the context of supply chain operations
3. The use of external data sources: the supply chain must or should be reviewed by recognized logistic professionals within the field

In this manner, the use and establishment of standards, policies and guidelines associated with logistics operations can be seen as being credible by other supply chain operators and industry professionals. Likewise, reliability of supply chain data is a quality that can be established through the development of targeted standards. Hence, supply chain data and information can, in this type of environment, be taken to represent what it is said to represent in terms of product, item status and unit disposition and so forth. Standards and guidelines can be developed as a means to minimize any potential errors in the global supply chain by ensuring that all logistics data is equally well documented.

CHAPTER VIII
The Internet of Things for Industry

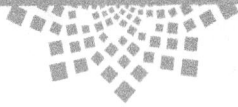

The logistics field has benefited, in many ways, much more than the rest of society and industry has from the extreme technological advances of the past 3 decades. Especially over the past decade. The logistics industry is one that benefits from the generation and use of data across a range of different functions and activities. In prior eras, before the development of electrical circuitry and miniaturization of integrated circuits, the generation and collection of data in the logistics industry was largely a labor-intensive procedure. Often a logistics operator's networked devices strategy is nothing more than a supply chain business' attempt to build a relationship with the logistics operator's products and services and this aspect still rests with executive leadership today.[60] IOT inherently supports such integrated relationship building by facilitating the deep connections in data that arise through networked environments:

Figure 24: Smart Supply Chain Components

This degree of networked connections is a reference to the smart supply chain which is really what the IOT provides. However, in the current environment networked devices making up the IOT have been appropriated by information and technology or IT applications and products designed to automate device technology in any given logistics operator. Most supply chain companies are rushing to automate and better manage all the ways they have traditionally dealt with products and services. This is including potential clients who might not be considering the movement products and services yet. Supply chain firms are also working to develop completely new concepts in managing the supply chain customer from a service perspective as well.

Networked device applications incorporate the business functions of any firm but certainly of logistics companies. These include those activities such as marketing, developing and maintaining customer and client shipping histories, and coordinating a logistics operator's multi-faceted approach to interactions with its clients and products and services. One important observation among the recent deluge of networked device applications in the supply chain environment is that the information and technology field is still in development and systems integration is an overriding concern. The technology meant to facilitate this degree of integration across a logistics operator's business processes, systems, and networks is being approached from a variety of different perspectives. These varying perspectives involve the different modalities displayed in the image below:

Table 7: Data Populating Supply Chains

Customers	Sales order information	IoT sensors
Carrier	Carrier location and item tracking	IoT sensors
Logistics Center	3-tier hierarchy (serial numbers, carton & pallet ID #s)	IoT sensors & readers
Direct Fulfillment	Product and unit configurations & information	IoT sensors & readers
Contract Manufacturers	Product assembly genealogies	Data logging & tracking
Suppliers	Component and sub-assembly lots	IoT sensors & readers

As this figure reveals, IOT data spans the gamut of connectivity within the supply chain. In essence, without a networked environment, the internet and data generating sensors the IOT would, of course, not exist at all. Therefore, these differing perspectives include those such as knowledge management and this in itself is making integration of IOT all the more complex structures. Clearly the underlying technology that supports networked device applications is in a state of perpetual development.

However, as these advances in technology have continued apace, so too has the ability of the logistics and supply chain industries to integrate data into a comprehensive, global network of interconnected data points. Logistics is, after all, also about the movement and strategic placement of data as it relates to the materials being transported within a supply chain. No data or poor data and untimely data all amount to product shrink, loss and/or damage up and down the entire supply chain. The most significant manifestation of this development involves the Internet of Things as it is referred to or IOT. The IOT has become a vast global array of interconnected devices that span not only one logistics provider's operations but rather spans up and down the entire supply chain. This IOT includes sensors and devices meant to manage entire supply chains to sensors and devices that are meant solely for a single node in a supply chain such as a truck and trailer, rail car or warehouse and so forth. At each node of the supply chain and virtually at all points in between, some form of data is being generated through the various devices, sensors and readers that populate the IOT.

The Internet and the World Wide Web (web) have permanently altered the way that societies the world over function. This radical change in function has also had a significant effect on logistics and supply chain management (SCM). One particular form of technology that is fundamentally supported by the Internet and the web is what is loosely described as the aforementioned Internet of Things or IOT. On the retail side the IOT consists of certain appliances such as refrigerators, washers and so forth that are connected to a network via the web. However, on the commercial side such as within the logistics field, the IOT consists of connected equipment such as robotic technology, automated product selectors, drones, self-driving vehicles and so on that are all coordinated via the web. Some research has already begun to recognize just how vast the IOT is and will become in the very near future. One study indicates that there are in excess of 15 billion unique devices connected across the existing IOT and that this figure will surpass 50 billion by 2020 alone which corresponds with the expectation of growth and diversity embodied in the Vision 2030.[61] In essence, the Vision 2030 ideals may be achievable without the advantages of IOT but the speed at which they will be achieved will be much faster with IOT support across the logistics sector in the Kingdom.

Because networked device technology and related applications reach into so many areas of a supply chain company's business, a networked device system is not normally a business solution that can be implemented out of the box per se Likewise, it could be said to require some degree of technology customization. Automating networked devices is an ongoing process for any logistics operator but certainly so in the supply chain industry where shipping companies, ports, and other service providers have constantly shifting demands on resources.[62] Additionally, a single vendor of networked device software applications may have difficulty meeting all the networking needs of a larger logistics operator. This is an explanation of the age-old rule that many supply chain operators and certainly many manufacturers, suppliers and retailers as well all subscribe to which is that a firm should never rely on a single vendor for anything. Doing so risks damage to one's own business should that single supplier or vendor develop problems with manufacturing, production or supply among other potential issues. Single vendors or suppliers are nice to have because cost efficiencies can be garnered from them that might not be available from multiple vendors due to quantity or volume ordering and supply. This is the efficiencies of scale that almost all businesses seek in their operations and supply chain operators are certainly no different than any other commercial enterprise.

The IOT is, at its core, an expression of a supply chain operator's existing technology infrastructure in one respect or another. Basically, a supply chain operator that has not invested heavily in IT will have great difficulty at leveraging the IOT for its core business processes. Likewise, those supply chain operators that have invested consistently in their IT infrastructure will find that leveraging the IOT almost occurs organically. Furthermore, a sophisticated IOT requires substantial effort on the part of a supply chain company's related departments. IOT enabled departments are able to ensure that the company's data is collected and updated regularly. Networked device systems traditionally focus on such areas as accounts, customer or client service, and shipping automation where accounts might include:[63]

- Accounts in the field
- Call center-based communications
- Supply chain and shipping interactions
- Supply chain processes

and customer service functions might be:

- Field service functions as well as dispatching
- Web-based services and client web-sites
- Call centers that encompass web-based shipping inquiries including email

while marketing automation functionalities might include:

- Data gathering tools
- Database support and management
- Data analysis
- Content management applications

Networked devices within the context of the IOT are simply not a single type of application. The IOT is both managed by a unique program platform as well as a mix of related applications.

The reason for this close relationship between the Saudi Vision 2030 and the IOT within the logistics field is that technology is seen as being central to achieving many if not most of the objectives found within the Vision (the core objectives of the Vision 2030 can be found in the Appendices section of this book). The Vision 2030 has as one of its underlying themes the intention to completely alter and improve the technical architecture within the Kingdom and of course this coincides precisely with the fundamental elements found within the IOT as it involves the supply chain. The point that should be stressed in this number of interconnected devices and sensors within the logistics IOT is that the generation and collection of data improves productivity, quality and accuracy all through the same capital investment in technology resulting in massive cost-leveraging within the supply chain as seen in the image below:

Figure 25: Growth of the IOT

INTERNET OF THINGS

In the early 1990s just when the internet was becoming more widespread, only a mere fraction of the value of material being managed by the IOT was taking place. Flash forward to today, where billions of dollars US are being managed via IOT enabled processes in the contemporary supply chain.

Basically, the IOT is a collection of devices, hardware or applications that are connected through a shared web-based network. In turn, these shared web-based networked applications, devices and sensors are subsequently coordinated in order to improve all of their processes or to actually support entirely new processes. For instance, one specific IOT application in the logistics and supply chain field can be found in warehouse forklift technology that acts to connect each facility forklift to the logistics technology platform via GPS. This IOT application applied to facility material movement and transportation can reduce a warehouse's operating costs by more than 10% by ensuring that forklifts are where they are needed more rapidly. Consequently, the IOT might be seen as an umbrella type of technology that integrates other emergent supply chain technologies in some regard. As the technology has developed, it became more apparent that sensors of one type or another could effectively be connected to a company's network. In effect, the backbone of the IOT is the cloud in which all the data, all the information and all the communications that collectively populate the supply chain are held in servers outside of a single supply chain operator as the figure below illustrates:

Figure 26: IOT Elements in the Supply Chain

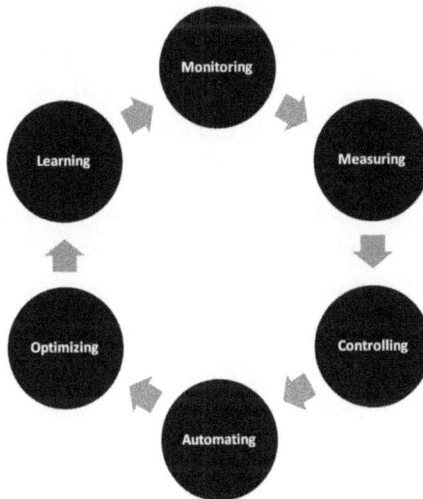

As this figure above demonstrates, it is the flow of data and information up and down the supply chain that fosters the real advantages found within the IOT. The IOT encourages the use of sensors and devices to measure and communicate with the network because it is this high level of interconnectivity that supply chain firms can leverage as a means to improve supply chain effectiveness, productivity and accuracy.

Thus, when first integrating a networked device system in the form of the IOT, a logistics operator must review the business processes that it intends on automating. This includes applications and technologies it may use to deal with products and services and develop a strategy to reengineer those specific processes in advance.[64] It should also be noted that a logistics operator must consider its schedule, its budgets and what its core objectives from deploying a networked devices application. Networked devices used to be centered almost solely on a variety of IT technologies and applications where customer service was the primary product of such centers. Yet, with the increasing dominance of the Internet, the Web, networks and other technology platforms, shipping companies have discovered they could more readily keep many of these networked devices functions in-house.

Although each individual sensor, data reader and connected device must function appropriately, overall it is management of this data independently of each sensor or device that creates the competitive advantage in the IOT for logistics operators. For instance, within port operations, the IOT creates a highly sophisticated nexus of data and information which directly influences how well container traffic is managed into and out of the port facilities by sea and land. The Port of Hamburg for example has implemented a smartPORT technology platform based on the IOT in which it uses 300 sensors on its roadways to monitor and control truck traffic delivering and picking up containers, installed digital signal devices to manage traffic flows, and integrated radar technology and RFID signals as a means to manage container vessel movement.[65] Hence, the IOT has led the Port of Hamburg to be able to improve traffic flows for transportation vehicles into and out of the port which in turn reduces pickup and delivery times. Yet, it also works to reduce fuel consumption by these port vehicles and trucking companies while also reducing overall wear and tear on the port roadways as well as city roadways by or near the port.

Such efficiencies throughout the entire supply chain achieved through the IOT has major implications not only for the Vision 2030 and the Kingdom's port facilities but for all of the Kingdom's economic cities.[66] For instance, supply chain development and the management of the supply chain is extremely important to the efficiency of any industrial center like Jubail Industrial City and the Kingdom's Ras Alkhair site as well. Jubail alone has an overall population that presently exceeds 100 thousand individuals. However, the economic center that Jubail supports accounts for more than 7% of Saudi Arabia's overall GDP which means that any efficiencies gained in the supply chain industry tends to have outsized impact across all industrial sectors. Furthermore, the workforce in just Jubail has grown to more than 50 thousand workers and the economic center's most recent growth phase referred to as Jubail II is responsible for adding another industrial complex with more than 22 primary industries each with their own unique logistics needs. These economic producing entities in tandem with already supporting what is the single largest petroleum company in the world ensures that logistics and supply chain industries are at the center of not just Jubail and Ras Alkhair's success but, indeed, the success of all of the Kingdom's economic cities. This is why it is argued that the IOT specifically ensures that the logistics industry in Saudi Arabia is perfectly aligned with the Vision 2030 objectives.

The massive movement of consumer products into and out of these two industrial cities relies on the efficient and cost-effective design of the global supply chain. This is the global supply chain that services all of Saudi Arabia's economic centers. These economic centers have all been designed from the ground up in some regard as a means to support a wide range of different commercial activities that all require an interconnected supply chain. The production and collection of data across these supply chains is a critical aspect of their long-term success and relevance to the Kingdom's Vision 2030 ideals. To this end, all of these cities have world-class ports such as the Jubail Commercial Seaport, the King Fahd Industrial Seaport, a private but small airport identified as Jubail Airport and a land bridge railway that is in progress now. Combined, all of these factors illustrate how critical the IOT is to supply chain design and management within the Kingdom.

The production and collection of data has become one of the most important technology applications in the contemporary logistics environment. The IOT and data analysis refer to the same logistics application. Essentially, the IOT is a reference to the strategic use of database driven technologies that support the collecting, analysis and protection of enormous amounts of data measured in terabytes which allows logistics firms to gain market insights for competitive advantage.[67] There is no one single IOT application or platform although the fundamental architecture remains the same regardless of the specific IOT application. The intrinsic architecture of IOT platforms is displayed in the table below:[68]

Table 8: IOT Architectures

The IOT Components	Supporting Technology Services
System Interface (GUI) and Applications	User Logins
Interfaces for Database Access and Analytic Programs	User Functionality
Databases for Operations and Logistical Data	Data Collection and Warehouses
Scalability for Cross-Platform Use	Encryption of Universal Data Formats
Data Streaming Capability and ETL Processing Functionality	Networking Functionality
External Sources of Data and External Data Sinks	Data Feeds

As this table illustrates, the IOT architecture is designed to support data collection, analysis and security. However, other features of the IOT separate it from traditional database designs and architecture within a more general business application.

The IOT applications are driven by certain qualities that were not available to prior iterations of database and data analysis applications prior to the rise of the cloud. These qualities are those that involve both accessibility, collection and application elements that were lacking, deficient or largely inconsistent in previous networked technologies. Presently, IOT applications are characterized by their ability to go out and collect data across different systems and to make use of this data more rapidly which are summarized as the four Vs of the IOT: a) volume of data collected, b) variety of data collected, c) velocity at which data is collected, and d) value of the data collected. These are the qualities that separate the IOT from a traditional database oriented technology application. Data analysis provides logistics firms with what amounts to a unique insight into consumer or client needs as well as logistics performance attributes or technology data that they would otherwise not be aware of.

This chapter has worked to examine the phenomenon of the IOT which is also a manifestation of the cloud and cloud-based technology applications. The IOT was identified within this section as being a collective technology driven solution that utilizes data gathering, data storage and data analysis to identify performance oriented, data-driven and efficiency related information for supply chain operators. Although companies across many industries have been collecting and storing data for many years in a variety of ways, the IOT has been shown to be building on these existing architectures due to the volume, variety, velocity and value of the different forms of data now available to logistics firms.

The actual methodology that logistics firms employ in developing, selecting and deploying a specific IOT application varies extensively. This variance depends upon a logistics firm's internal competencies, its resources as well as its existing technology infrastructure. All logistics operators have some form of technology infrastructure in place and various aspects of this technology infrastructure is intended to interface with external technology platforms through universal data languages and processes. Research has demonstrated that the IOT applications do depend upon certain pre-existing capabilities within a firm. These include those such as data ingestion or how data is collected, data storage or how data is actually retained and then the analytics which is really the domain of the IOT platform itself within the cloud.[69] Logistics operators that maintain data in a universally recognized format but collect data that has no usefulness to external operators in essence defeat the purpose of universality. The first components of this model are essentially commoditized because logistics firms have been collecting data for many years and attempting to preserve this data in various forms. Therefore, when designing an effective logistics technology platform that is meant to function within the context of the IOT, both common data formats and common forms of data must be considered in advance of implementation.

However, the IOT is also a reference to the way in which the analysis of this existing data and the data that is now available across numerous networks is processed and managed. As the analysis and discussion in this chapter demonstrates, companies such as Wal-Mart, Carrefour and Target and other major retailers can really leverage the IOT for their own benefit. These types of firms have massive existing technology infrastructure available therefore can develop logistical models to leverage their the IOT applications. In contrast, companies that lack the technology infrastructure required to mine the supply chain in some respect can turn to IOT service firms in order to leverage their own in-house IOT applications.[70] Regardless of whether these types of IOT applications are developed through in-house technologies or acquired through third party providers, such IOT applications can result in a sustainable competitive advantage that is difficult for competitors to mimic within the logistics and supply chain field.

CHAPTER IX
Robotic Fulfillment Centers

The typical supply chain in the logistics field is made of a series of connected nodes of operation which are, increasingly, handled by robotic solutions. The use of robots has advanced so much throughout the world but certainly within the Kingdom that Saudi Arabia has become the first nation to grant a robot actual citizenship. In 2017 the Kingdom announced, in conjunction with its Neom City development, the granting of citizenship to Sophia, a humanoid robot built by Hansen Robotics.[71] However, on a topical level, a supply chain first is made of a series of functions that must be coordinated with each other in terms of forecasting demand. The forecasting of demand is in relation to material supply, adapting the supply chain to late stage changes in product designs such as those that arise in the Kingdom's logistics industry, and handling inventory shortages and slow moving products that result in increased returns. Hence, among the overall functions that must be considered in the design and management of an effective supply chain are the following: 1) research and development or R&D, 2) product design and development, 3) sales and marketing or S&M, 4) operations, 5) customer relationship management or CRM and, 6) corporate finances such as accounts payable, accounts receivable and income accounting.[72] Each of these functions within a supply chain operator must be integrated into the design and management of the supply chain operator's logistics operations.

Traditional fulfillment centers within the supply chain have relied primarily on human labor in order to pick, pack and ship products. This is now changing with the rapid development of robotic fulfillment centers that have largely automated these processes. Robotic fulfillment centers employ robots which may be free traveling robots that move through self-tracking methods around a warehouse facility or robots that move on predetermined tracks from selection points to the shipping point. These types of robotics may seem mundane by sci-fi standards or standards in other industries where robots perform highly sophisticated activities but they are still enormously effective at minimizing the need for human workers:

Figure 27: Robotic Fulfilment Centers

Simply being able to remove the need for human workers to walk to various points within a warehouse and carry products away is extremely efficient. Additionally, some fulfillment centers now utilize drones which are, functionally, robots to select some products as well because such drone technology allows them to go higher up in storage space without the added infrastructure development for robotic lifts. Regardless, firms such as

Amazon Robotics, LLC, formerly Kiva and Locus Robotics now offer fulfillment robot technology that almost completely automate the small form factor product fulfillment process. It is these types of industry benchmarks that can attract the necessary foreign investment in the economic cities at the heart of the Vision.

In terms of Amazon Robotics for instance, Amazon's robots, formerly Kiva, almost all of Amazon's robot production is directed inward. Amazon's various global fulfilment centers are using in excess of 30,000 of these robotic fulfillment machines in order to meet its own internal demand.[73] Newly developing competitors to Amazon Robotics in the supply chain are now opening up endless opportunities to supply chain automation. One area being developed is the area of autonomous mobile robotics or AMR which focuses on actually moving products and materials to the end-consumer or end-user of the item. Hence, while the supply chain operators themselves often are not involved in product design and development, they are affected by these types of issues to be sure. This arises since such aspects as inventory levels and shipping costs are related to these product or material related concerns. In terms of the actual nodes of operations that most typical supply chains operate, these are more commonly recognized as supply chain or logistics operations that, in fact, can be automated to one degree or another. These interconnected nodes are usually described as being: vendors, suppliers, manufacturers or producers, distribution firms, warehouse and inventory facilities, and the supply chain operators themselves. Within each of these various operators, the opportunity to automate exists in virtually each operational category.

These nodes directly relate to the creation and movement of consumer product goods from the manufacturer or producer to the supply chain operators' areas of operation. These areas of operation include those such as warehouses or transportation equipment and, ultimately, to the end consumer. The end consumer has no idea the level of robotic automation that has been involved in their product selection, shipment and overall fulfillment. At any rate, automating the movement of an item from the warehouse shelf is the first step in fulfillment within the supply chain. As such, it is this transaction process in the fulfilment center supported by robotic technology that basically presents the single greatest point for automation within the logistics and supply chain sector:

Figure 28: Fulfilment Center Robot

This particular task is one that can siphoned off to a fully automated machine or robot which can be controlled remotely. The entire fulfilment system can be managed much as a water hose in terms of volume such that customization of fulfilment can be achieved as a means to respond to market conditions further down the supply chain. This entire supply chain is actually referred to in the industry as a commodity chain in which raw materials are integrated into the supply and distribution of consumer product goods to the end user or the consumer.[74] All of these functional areas and operational nodes comprise the supply chain within the logistics field. The logistics field is one in which any form of variance is viewed as a negative because it directly interferes with the efficient delivery of a product to the distributor or end consumer. Thus, automation in the form of robotics is actually a positive with respect to the marketplace of things.

An effective supply chain is really just a metaphor for making full use of a supply chain operator's internal capacities and operating capabilities. Retail growth and expansion relies on the establishment of an economic rationale not only in terms of overall revenues from sales but also in terms of operating efficiency and operating margins such as supply chain operators and clients do in the Kingdom. The logistics firms and their clients in the Kingdom's economic cities must accurately forecast their product lead-times in order to balance factors such as seasonality, loss, shrinkage and damage while still being able to minimize inventory carrying costs. These operating margins that provide the rationale for growth are an expression of supply chain efficiency in terms of capacity utilization. All of these factors are facilitated through the implementation of automation or robotics at virtually all points in the typical supply chain. The fact remains that the capacity to make and produce a good or service often requires a series of fixed operating costs. When the demand for a given product or service is seen as low, capacity within the supply chain becomes underutilized and the subsequent total unit costs tend to increase. Likewise, when the demand for a given product or service increases, the output can be pushed to higher levels as a response to demand but the supply chain must have the ability to manage this capacity. This capacity utilization is a characteristic in which over-utilization produces bottlenecks and excess inventory levels. Such outcomes lead to too much capital being tied up in product as it moves through a supply chain operator's supply chain. These issues are completely avoidable through the implementation and use of robotics in the supply chain.

The fulfilment center in particular has become what amounts to a newer category within the logistics and supply chain industries. While major distribution centers have always been around since the age of mass production, distribution and retail began, the concept of a fulfillment center that essentially bypasses the retail segment of the supply chain is somewhat novel still. Of course, Amazon dominates this logistics category in terms of size and volume but many other logistics operators, retailers and service providers have moved into this logistics category. In essence, major fulfilment centers can be anywhere from 300,000 square feet to more than a million square feet and 3rd party logistics providers, big-box retailers and of course online retailers have all established fulfillment centers over the past decade in which automation, robotics and technology are the secret sauce that makes these centers work.[75] Automation can be active from the order/item selection to the movement of the item to the loading/shipping point without a human worker ever actually touching an item. Furthermore, as these fulfilment centers become ever more automated, the technology within them has the capacity to be applied externally within the civic apparatus in which the fulfillment centers themselves are located.

It is this element of technological transfer that makes robotics in the fulfillment center application so attractive to the Kingdom and its Vision 2030 ideals. The Vision 2030 is an economic, technological and cultural set of initiatives which must all be achieved simultaneously in order for the Crown Prince's Vision to be realized. This symbiosis between robotic fulfillment center technology and civic apparatus is evident in the Jazan City For Primary And Downstream Industries which not only maintains key fulfillment centers for retailers but also employs logistics operations in its port facilities as well as city maintenance activities that are prime targets for automation such as street sweepers, supply depots and traffic semaphores and so on. All of these symbiotic elements in the robotic fulfillment center and the civic apparatus of the city are evident in the following image:[76]

Figure 29: Robotic Fulfilment Center Elements

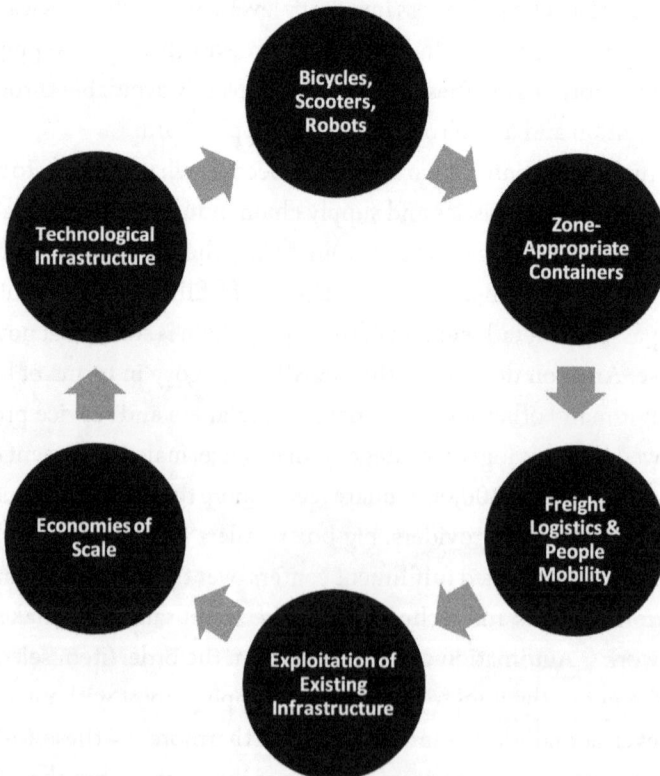

It is clear that robotic equipment is ideally suited for completing many of the routine and mundane tasks that any municipality is faced with on a daily basis. Yet, most municipalities lack the finances or the expertise to either purchase off the shelf solutions or to develop their own unique robotic applications. Yet, the Jazan City For Primary And Downstream Industries and other economic cities within the Kingdom have a close, symbiotic relationship with the industries that populate these cities and thus the transference of such technology is entirely achievable as part of the Vision 2030 objectives.

Over-utilization ensures that other inefficiencies occur related to operations of the supply chain. For instance as excess man-hours and other resources such as transportation costs contribute to operational losses or narrower operating margins at best for a logistics provider. Likewise, under-utilization of supply chain capacity ensures that resources are equally as wasted and this type of scenario is especially evident when manufacturers, for instance, introduce radical production methodologies into the Kingdom's economic cities which emphasize technological innovation, efficiency building and economies of scale. This type of logistics automation methodology requires components to be functional at production, distribution and transportation. Thus it is or can be difficult for logistics managers to accurately assess raw material requirements which can affect the amount of material in the overall supply chain. Essentially, supply chain officers and managers are tasked with the responsibility to adjust supply chain capacity based on such factors as seasonality, demand, artificial events such as weather events, as well as competitive pressures as such factors lead to a shift in the cost per unit of products. Automation in the form of robotics in the supply chain responds to these needs. Supply chain design, supply chain management, and distribution operations form a critical competitive aspect of any supply chain operator's operations with robotics now at the forefront of logistics technology considerations.

CHAPTER X
Self-Driving Vehicles

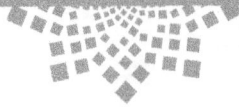

The past several years has seen an rapid advance in the development of self-driving vehicle technology. This self-driving vehicle technology is largely enabled through the widespread access to GPS mapping, real-time data tracking and robotic technology on vehicle platforms. Self-driving vehicle technology is being led by companies such as Google's Waymo and its self-driving car technology, Uber's Otto system for truck automation and finally Tesla's Autopilot software and sensors. Additionally, in some sense, the FSS and similar container transportation technologies are an expression of self-driving vehicle technology as well. Self-driving vehicles run the gamut from small, automated carts within warehouse facilities to the larger railcar and truck technology that delivers large containers. Regardless of the particular form factor of an automated, self-driving vehicle, the important consideration is that a human operator is not necessary or is an operational afterthought.

Google is one of the companies currently leading the development of automated vehicles surprisingly enough because Google is as far from a car company or a transportation company as a company could be. And yet, if one is speaking of a digitized world where the physical environment is constantly being measured in terms of data, Google might be one of the firms most competent to develop a self-driving, fully automated vehicle:

Figure 30: Google's Self-Driving Platform

Google uses its automated vehicles to expand its mapping software applications. It also uses these vehicles to navigate the communities, roadways and structures that populate the earth and then integrates these images and GPS data into its mapping, topographical and imaging applications like Google Earth in the online environment.

Innovative electric vehicle companies such as Tesla are now not only developing electric vehicles, autonomous vehicles but also electric, autonomous trucks intended to revolutionize the transportation industry. Tesla in particular has been one technology firm that has introduced a paradigm shift into the autonomous, alternative energy vehicle category. Tesla's innovative business strategy meant that it came to market with an electric vehicle platform but almost as an afterthought introduced autonomous vehicle technology into its cars over the past several years. The company's autonomous vehicle platform is called Autopilot and it is based on technology framework referred to as the Advanced Driver Assist System or ADAS. In a departure from other major manufacturers of autonomous vehicles, Tesla does not utilize LIDAR technology within its cars because of the cost factor but instead relies on a series of 8 individual cameras which create a full 360 degrees of vision combined with some 12 ultrasonic sensors for parameter information and forward-looking radar.[77] These sensory inputs are managed by Autopilot and its ADAS platform to produce cars that can pilot themselves, that can learn over time and that are being constantly updated remotely by the firm.

An now, this technology combined with LIDAR is being leveraged by Tesla in the all-important transportation and logistics sector. Tesla's heavy duty semi-truck platform an all-electric vehicle running on its established modular lithium ion battery cells that are typically placed horizontally along the frame of the vehicle. Additionally, his semi-trucks are designed to be aerodynamically more efficient than the typical diesel powered vehicle and to employ LED lighting, self-charging technology and, of course, autonomous piloting because of the often fixed routes that the logistics industry requires.[78] Tesla's shift into the autonomous transportation sector is indicative of how the standard down-cycle supply chain moves in terms of innovation. This movement is typically in a unidirectional path which usually means from the manufacturer or producer to the retailer and then to the consumer. These types of standard supply chains move CPGs in mass shipments within the logistics industry that substantially reduce the cost of such shipments on a per item basis. This leads to the economies of scale that autonomous trucks such as Tesla's can take advantage of vis-à-vis fixed routes. Still, within in some industries this type of per item or per unit cost as well as the entire problem of factors such as reverse logistics must be dealt with in a completely different way. Utilities industries are an example of the novelty which can be applied to different industries in this regard because they have invested in infrastructure that actually allows the consumer to sell electricity back to the utility and move this excess capacity back up the supply chain.[79] While the type of product facilitates this particular solution, the concept can be and should be applied to every industry with respect to the logistics industry. The outcome is such that this downward movement of CPGs and other products is largely automated and transparent, from a data perspective, all along the supply chain and decision nodes regarding product inventory and resource supply levels. Such inventory levels, capacities and movement of goods can be built into the logistics transportation system and autonomous vehicles facilitate this type of design.

The actual cost of processing returned CPGs and products can actually surpass the costs of incoming items on a per-unit basis within the typical supply chain. Thus, autonomous vehicles offer a solution to not only fully automate fixed transportation routes at lower costs but also improve the functional processes that comprise reverse logistics as well. The fact is that the delivery back to a distributor or producer can take as long as one to the three months in some cases. Yet, these types of costs must be dealt with in an economic fashion because of the huge amount of goods, $2 to $3 hundred billion for North America alone by some estimates, are moved back up the supply chain for instance.[80] Therefore, logistics operators can hardly ignore product returns although many of them have been hesitant to commit the necessary resources to adequately address such returns. Yet, with the advent of autonomous vehicles the issue of reverse logistics becomes much more manageable. In effect, reverse logistics supply chains are closed loop systems which benefit from autonomous operations. While there is certainly still a cost factor associated with acquiring autonomous vehicles, with solutions such as Tesla's semi-truck platform, closed loop supply chains are now much more achievable and affordable from a commercial application perspective. The consumer and retail sector has developed some of the most important technology solutions that are used within the logistics industry and autonomous vehicles are a good example of this technology transfer from one sector to another.

One practical issue relating to autonomous vehicles, commercial or otherwise, involves the regulatory aspect of the technology and the application. In the US and other major development markets, there are federal motor vehicle standards relating to safety, efficiency and licensing among others that must be complied with. These regulations are nationally mandated and offer minimum standards which means that autonomous vehicle manufacturers have to build higher tolerances into their platforms relating to the following framework:[81]

- 100 Level: Avoidance of impending accidents: this regulation relates to the autonomous vehicle controls, displays and the shifting lever mechanism along with all of the vehicle's hydraulic systems including its braking system. The regulation also relates to the mirrors, accelerator control and operation along with lights, warning systems and alerts.
- 200 Level: Worthiness in crashes: the protection of the vehicle occupants and cargo relating to the effectiveness of body and head

restraints, air bags, glass glazing technology, door locking operations, the inclusion of side impact solutions and roof crush structure
supports.

- 300 Level: Fuel System Safety: the fuel system of all vehicles must
resist post-crash operation, vehicle materials must be rated for flam-
mability and alternative fuels such as natural gas and similar must
have appropriate safety applications.
- 400 Level: Autonomous Vehicle Regulations: All technology systems must be validated by an independent safety commission, fail-
safes must be integrated into all systems, cyber-security issues must
be addressed, long-term reliability of technology systems must be
established, autonomous system sensors must be universally read-
able and their operation must be integrated into first responder
training.

Thus, autonomous vehicles can and should conform to the fundamental
safety and operational standards that all vehicles must comply with in these
regulated markets. Additionally, there has to be the development and inclusion of specific standards targeting autonomous vehicle systems alone. This
is because the sheer differences between regular vehicles and autonomous
vehicles are very extreme in character.

Autonomous vehicles consist of a technology platform as well as a logistics resolution. The very concept of autonomous operations in vehicles
and trucks requires communicative networks to exist which bind them
all together as well as connects them to a host of other types of data networks. This all-encompassing kind of network is based on the concept of
vehicle-to-vehicle communication and vehicle-to-technology infrastructure
communication. This is one potential resolution to resolve the data compatibility and vulnerability issues with sensor based autonomous vehicle
technology. Autonomous technology communication involves connecting
all the vehicles and infrastructure elements such as traffic lights, road signs
and other transportation system data through wide area network or WAN
technology. Such WAN systems would operate under the targeted 5GHz
frequency bandwidth in order not generate interference with other roadway
and transportation related communication signals.[82] Through the autonomous technology communication network, vehicles and infrastructures

can emit signals and essentially communicate with each other resulting in autonomous vehicles that would know what events are occurring around them. Some potential functions that would be facilitated through autonomous technology communication networks such as this includes vehicle breakdown warnings, inclement weather alerts, pre and post-crash alerts as well as traffic related advisories.[83] Vehicles connected to autonomous technology communication will be able to send and receive these types of messages and process them rapidly in order to prevent accidents and/or variations in routes from occurring.

The autonomous technology communication will essentially improve and supplement the current autonomous vehicle platforms being developed for the logistics sector. For instance, in the scenario of an unforeseen vehicle breakdown, the sensor based autopilot systems will be programmed to only react after the sensors determine what has happened. This means that the amount of time provided to the surrounding vehicles on the roadway to adjust themselves around the disabled transportation vehicle is somewhat limited. Yet, if the surrounding vehicles were able to be notified of what is happening to one vehicle in advance then they can actually make adjustments to avoid the impending route problems sure to occur. The ways in which regular vehicles and autonomous vehicles compare vis-à-vis their operational characteristics are displayed in the figure below:[84]

Table 9: Autonomous Vehicle Complexity Chart

Level 0	Level 1	Level 2	Level 3	Level 4	Level 5
No Autonomy	Assisted Autonomy	Partial Autonomy	Conditional Autonomy	High Autonomy	Full Autonomy
Human Operated	Human Operation with Velocity & Steering Assistance	Human Monitoring of All Functions	Human is a Functional Fail-Safe	Human Operator May Undertake Other Non-Driving Tasks	No Human Operator Presence

As the figure demonstrates, non-autonomous vehicles depend solely upon the input and judgment of the vehicle operator. As automation is increased incrementally, the vehicle operator receives some data and information from the vehicle sensors and is expected to make adjustments based on this data and information. As the level of automation increases, the vehicle system begins to integrate the self-generated data and information and make adjustments to the vehicle operation itself. Of course, as the system complexity and sophistication increases, the need for a vehicle operator decreases to the point where one is not necessary at all from a technological and operational perspective.

Regardless of the specific format or the particular application, self-driving vehicle technology incorporates certain similar technology applications. One of the core applications at the center of any self-driving vehicle platform is LIDAR or light detection and ranging technology which utilizes laser pulses to capture and assess distances between objective s, develop three-dimensional imagery and topographical feedback. LIDAR instrumentation incorporates both a laser and GPS along with specialized scanners that allow the technology to control the necessary inputs into vehicle management depending on the actual vehicle application. In practical application such as Uber's self-driving truck technology, LIDAR is used in tandem with high-definition cameras, traditional radar and onboard computers to actually pilot the truck over freeways and roadways. It is estimated that some 70% of all freight movement within the supply chain is moved, at some point, by trucks and thus being able to essentially automate this entire transportation process would make this network exponentially more efficient. Considering that the JAZAN CITY FOR PRIMARY AND DOWNSTREAM INDUSTRIES is still in its earlier developmental stages, utilizing this type of cutting edge logistics technology means that the economic centers driving the Vision can forward integrate emerging technologies.

Autonomous vehicles have the capacity to revolutionize the supply chain as well as industry in general. This revolutionary change is the equivalent of a complete paradigm shift in the marketplace as well. Autonomous vehicles simply function in a completely different way that traditional vehicles with respect to transportation, operation and design. The information discussed thus far reveals that within the Kingdom, autonomous vehicles are actually synergistic with the objectives of the Vision 2030 because of autonomous vehicle technology's capacity to automate the movement of goods and services. These synergies are presented in the bullet points below:

- Efficiencies: The Vision seeks improve household savings from 6 to 10% with respect to incomes
  o Autonomous vehicles are certain improve GDP allowing citizens to earn more while spending less
- Regulatory Effectiveness: The Vision has the objective ive in mind to elevate government revenues from SAR163 billion to more than SAR1 trillion
  o Autonomous vehicles can move more products less expensively than traditional methods leading to efficiencies of scale
- Private Sector Contribution: The Vision intends to elevate the private sector's contribution to the national economy from 40% to 65% of overall GDP
  o Autonomous vehicles improve both a firm's gross revenues as well as its operating margins leading to collective gains in GDP
- Foreign Direct Investment: The Vision means to improve foreign direct investment from 3.8% to at least 5.7% of national GDP
  o Autonomous vehicles that are integrated into the national transportation system offer international firms a sustainable competitive advantage relative to long-term costs

Hence, it is evident that autonomous vehicles are not only the way of the future but that the future is now for the Kingdom. Where other countries and markets may have invested too much in their existing transportation infrastructure systems to consider alternative approaches, the Kingdom is in the unique position of being able to develop autonomous transportation systems from the ground up in its economic centers.

EPILOGUE
Enacting the Vision

The top ten logistics trends discussed in this book are all driven, in one respect by the need for and the presence of innovation. Innovation, whether fueled by technology or the effects of technology, ensures that companies in all industries but certainly within the logistics and supply chain industries are able to remain relevant over the long-term. These top ten trends are really a manifestation of the influence that innovation has on commerce in the marketplace and is really a testament to the theory of innovation embodied within the innovation standard paradigm. The innovation standard paradigm is a concept currently in play within many commercial enterprises throughout the world. Tesla is a company that is discussed in some depths in several of the chapters in this book and its CEO, Elon Musk, could be said to have embraced the innovation standard paradigm. Several developments being implemented by Tesla as a corporation are indicative of just how powerful this paradigm can be for the logistics sector as Tesla's introduction of its semi-truck product reveals:

Figure 31: Tesla's Market Leading Move into Electric

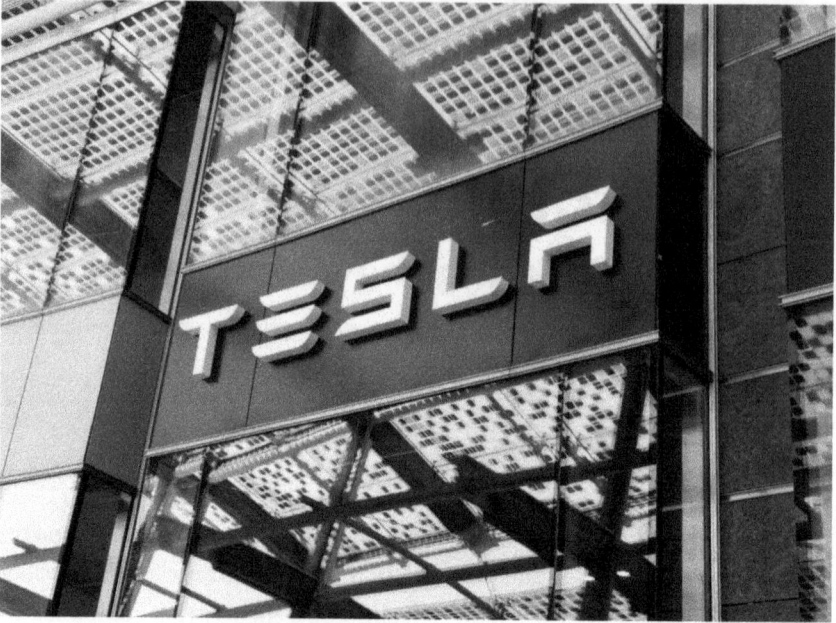

Innovation for Musk and his company, Tesla, is driven by design or rather intention. It could be argued in this sense that Tesla is not necessarily in the electric vehicle business or in the alternative energy business but rather in the innovation business.

The innovation standard paradigm is one in which newer innovations typically allow the respective companies that adopt them to thrive. Such innovations allow competitors within particular industries to succeed while the incumbents in these same industries are weighted down with what is then inefficient technologies. This perspective is one which mirrors the product life cycle to some extent. This is because as new products and services, which are often based on technological innovations themselves, are introduced they have a substantial growth curve before their subsequent maturity and then decline sets in. Thus, technical innovation and growth in any industry is generally accomplished through a variety of strategies that relate to phenomenon of technological innovation.

Additionally, technical innovation within an enterprise is typically characterized as being achieved in one of several ways. Typically these are viewed as being due to organic activities made through in-house efforts or alternatively accomplished through mergers and acquisitions (M&A) or other external means. In determining an incumbent logistics company's objectives and strategic deliverables, an incumbent logistics company's leadership must first decide on what type of technical innovation would best support its growth strategies. This form of consideration usually requires identifying a particular market and determining how best to enter that market whether geographically based on product oriented. Purchasing a newer competitor with the most recent technological innovations in an industry in order to remain competitive is a mature logistics company's easiest method to achieve parity with newly innovative companies. That is, they establish a company's technical innovation plans relative to how the operations of the logistics company would be integrated into the operations would be an external technical innovation strategy. In all instances, innovation of both products/services and operations remains the focus of the firm and its executive leadership as well as of its employees.

Companies that are intent on rapid growth are usually younger companies. This arises because such younger firms need to expand in order to sustain their revenues and it is often the case younger firms have access to the newest technology and thus their growth is fueled by newer innovations. Thus, growth oriented companies are somewhat entrepreneurial in character and typically result in job growth in the markets in which they decide to expand. The outcome is that smaller and more entrepreneurial logistics companies will utilize different and more adaptive technology innovations than those associated with established logistics companies. Additionally, the directors and shareholders of these types of logistics companies are less risk averse than established companies. This in turn provides executive leadership in these logistics operators with substantially more strategic leeway in its decision-making capacity. Flexibility within the context of decision-making is a critical aspect of innovation and creativity in the first place it would seem. In terms of the technology innovations that these companies take then, they prefer strategies that provide them with greater degrees of control over logistics operations but perhaps less over that of their client firms' brands. These are business practices that established logistics companies with existing technology solutions and platforms can benchmark in order to remain relevant in supply chain industry.

However, the single most inhibiting element that keeps more innovative technologies such as AFS technology from broad logistics applications involves price of adoption. Furthermore, such price barriers also keep such innovative technologies from moving up the product lifecycle faster. The price tag that is often associated with new technologies can be inhibitive for first movers or early adopters. Even in a strong economic environment these products' cost for the logistics marketplace can be extremely high. In relation to AFS technology extremely so considering most logistics providers cannot yet replace the appropriate operations completely with a single AFS application. Since AFS technology costs roughly much more than existing technologies in many cases it makes little economic and logistical sense for the average logistics firm to invest completely in AFS technology right now. The outcome is that for the average logistics provider, AFS technology's cost ensures that the logistics consumer is faced with a technology choice still driven largely by the cost factor. This reality is clearly seen in the fact that the logistics marketplace has not embraced AFS technology as a new, innovative technology on a widespread basis despite its clear efficiencies. Furthermore, considering the volatility of fuel costs as well as periods of economic decline, AFS technology's cost is even more of a hindrance for broad market acceptance since low fuel prices still cyclically occur. These are all elements that typically affect any new, innovative technology and the young, immature companies in the logistics industry.

The conclusion is such that even though established logistics companies with less innovative technologies supporting their products and services may be at a technical disadvantage, they have certain innate advantages relative to their operations. The geographic location of a logistic company's suppliers and vendors is a critical consideration. This is so in not only a competitive advantage sense in developing a price or cost advantage but these existing networks can nullify any innovation advantage newer supply chain operators may have. Sourcing requirements and demands of additional client firms and markets can be difficult to meet in certain markets for younger logistics providers that are coming to market with differential advantages. What this means for logistics companies that are relying on established technologies is that they must develop a strategy that ensures that they benefit from the global marketplace. That is, they must learn to innovate in a manner that ensures that these expanding companies develop into a true multinational logistics provider. This would allow them to overcome the differential economic incentives that younger logistics companies have.

This development has led to even greater market innovation and integration between established logistics companies and their suppliers and contractors. This has developed to the point where many supply chain operators are now sharing logistics channels and even information and technology platforms to ensure that their line of businesses are fully integrated, updated with real-time accuracy, and shared operational risks. These types of strategies relative to achieving high efficiency levels require not only strategic planning but almost immediate action in the marketplace. Such immediacy of strategy implementation occurs because the pace of technological advances never stops. These technological advances ensure that logistics competitors small and large can establish market differentiation by utilizing these services and integrative capabilities equally well. As a result, this means that sourcing new and more adaptive logistics providers is necessary if a company is going to be able to meet expanded demand that comes when faced with new market entrants in their market of choice.

The development of a dependable and reliable supply chain is related to the geographic location of suppliers. However, if anything, it is even more critical for established logistics companies. Newer entrants with innovative technologies can also take advantage of these competencies as well. Yet, a logistics company that is expanding into a new market that develops the perfect technology strategy and has geographically convenient suppliers can still fail in its growth initiative. For instance, if such a logistics operator cannot get its products to market due to supply chain issues. A supply chain has been defined in this book as the sum of all the related retailers, product and raw material distributors, transportation solutions, storage warehouses, as well as supplier networks that contribute to a company's movement of products from production to the end-consumer. It is integrally related to an incumbent company's logistics and overall operations in that operations management oversees the smooth functioning of the logistics company's supply chain.

Younger, more innovative companies have often failed to develop the most efficient supply chains and operations. Thus, a supply chain that has supply delivery concerns such as bottlenecks, excessive inventory levels, or difficulties even sourcing products or services almost always results in a loss in revenue. Other negative outcomes related to these types of issues can be poor product or poor service quality metrics, and a loss of customers or clients, whether these are internal or external. For most established companies then, ensuring that their integrated distribution and logistics layers are functioning smoothly is directly relevant to their ability to remain competitive. Consequently, these types of considerations must be made or should be made prior to selecting a competitive strategy. For established logistics competitors, there are several strategies to ease these sorts of supply chain and logistics concentrations in order to make the system more responsive. However, these responsive strategies must be devised within the context of how an incumbent firm intends on competing within the selected market and on the character of the emerging technologies within that industry.

Currently, many logistics companies remain intent on technical innovation as a way to enter into new markets. Yet, at times such firms suffer primary strategic limitations associated with that technical innovation relative to their overall operations. The necessity of ensuring such elements within their supply chains can facilitate or support technical innovation places them at a distinct disadvantage to incumbent firms in the industry unless they actually partner with one. These elements relate to the limited number of suppliers for each of an incumbent logistics company's primary product lines in developed markets. This occurs since many suppliers have outsourced or off-shored some or all of their production or manufacturing to developing markets. In relation to core strategy development then, incumbent firms in a given industry may rely on their established technical infrastructure as a competitive advantage provided that they recognize it as such.

Essentially, there is room for both younger, more innovative logistics companies as well as older more established competitors. For Saudi Arabia and its Vision 2030, the contemporary global economy functions as the underlying pretext for a shift in how incumbent firm strategy is both formulated and makes use of the global markets vis-à-vis technical innovations. Most contemporary markets are associated with the rapid pace of technological development which involves the sheer speed at which logistics data, information, and supply chain knowledge pulse between logistics operators. In the contemporary business environment, fast logistics companies generate advantages and market presence while even faster ones generate more advantages and greater market power almost exponentially. While this observation might seem overly simplistic in some respects it also indicates how the gap between strategic planning and execution has virtually disappeared for many companies due to technological innovations now available. This change occurs regardless of whether a logistics company is an established one or a new entrant with the most recent technical innovations. The conclusion is that younger and more technologically innovative logistics companies do not automatically have a competitive advantage in the global marketplace. This relates to certain cost elements which often decide how competitive a logistics company is regardless of technological innovation but the clear consensus is that technological innovation is fueling growth in the industry. Such growth provides enormous economic upside for the Kingdom and is the underlying rationale contained within the Vision 2030 ideals.

APPENDICES

APPENDIX 1
Human Factor Effects of Supply Chain Technologies[85]

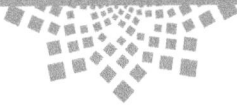

DEGREE OF AUTOMATION 2020-2050		INFORMATION ACQUISITION	INFORMATION ANALYSIS	DECISION & ACTION SELECTION	ACTION IMPLEMENTATION	OVERALL DoA
2020	HIGH	25.00%	31.25%	18.75%	12.50%	14.58%
	MODERATE	18.75%	0.00%	12.50%	18.75%	
	LOW	12.50%	12.50%	6.25%	6.25%	
2025	HIGH	30.00%	40.00%	20.00%	10.00%	15.83%
	MODERATE	20.00%	0.00%	10.00%	20.00%	
	LOW	10.00%	10.00%	15.00%	5.00%	
2030	HIGH	25.00%	33.33%	16.67%	8.33%	17.36%
	MODERATE	16.67%	0.00%	20.83%	29.17%	
	LOW	20.83%	20.83%	12.50%	4.17%	
2050	HIGH	26.92%	34.62%	19.23%	7.69%	18.59%
	MODERATE	15.38%	0.00%	23.08%	30.77%	
	LOW	23.08%	23.08%	11.54%	7.69%	
AVERAGE CHANGE 2020-2050		3.04%	4.65%	5.45%	2.88%	4.01%

APPENDIX 2
Performance Efficiencies Gained from SCM Technology

Performance Related Outcomes	Performance Types		
	Efficiency	Effectiveness	Adaptiveness
Reduce processing expenses	X		
Elevated equipment use		X	
Elevated planning process		X	
Elevated responsiveness			X
Facilitate decision making		X	
Elevated relationships with clients/vendors			X
Decrease number of administrative employees	X		
Reduction of product cycle times	X		
Increases in productivity	X		
Enhance intra-channel cooperation			X
Reduce product errors/loss/waste		X	

APPENDIX 3

Innovation Development in
the Logistics Industry[86]

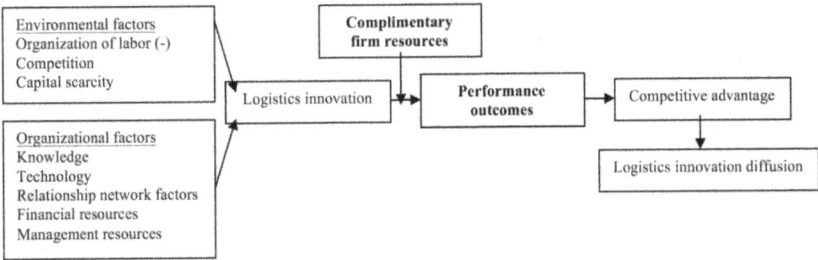

Environmental factors	Complimentary firm resources	
Organization of labor (-)		
Competition		
Capital scarcity		

Logistics innovation → Performance outcomes → Competitive advantage → Logistics innovation diffusion

Organizational factors
Knowledge
Technology
Relationship network factors
Financial resources
Management resources

APPENDIX 4
Saudi Vision 2030 Core Objectives

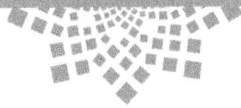

- Increase foreign direct investment (FDI) from 3.8% to 5.7% of GDP in line with more developed economies.
- Increase the private sector's GDP contribution from the present 40% to 65% by 2030, and, in particular, increase SME GDP contribution to 35% (from the present 20%).
- Decrease the overall rate of unemployment from the current 11.6% to just 7% by 2030 and improve the participation of women in the national workforce.
- Elevate government effectiveness and efficiency and improve Saudi Arabia's position in the Government Effectiveness Index (GEI) published by the World Bank. Saudi Arabia ranked 80th in 2015, and the government has the intention to increase this to at least 20th place as part of the Vision 2030.
- Improve Saudi Arabia's position on the annual Global Competitive Index published by the World Economic Forum (WEF). The government aims to be listed as one of the top 10 countries listed on the WEF index by 2030. The country ranks 25th at the time of publication.

Notes

a. Drones are appearing in a range of industries and fulfilling numerous roles within those industries. Thus, it comes as no surprise that drones are not only finding applicational uses within the logistics industry but are actually affecting dramatic changes in how many processes are done, what processes can be done and facilitating entirely new concepts in the industry.

b. Bottlenecks are extremely damaging to any supply chain and must be avoided at all costs. Bottlenecks result not only in delayed deliveries but also in the undue buildup of capital within the supply chain which undermines a business' entire business case. Too much capital in a supply chain ensures that businesses do not have access to working capital within other areas of their operations.

c. FSS applications are still in their infancy in terms of where and how they can be applied. FSS applications in particular require right-of-way considerations because of existing roadways, zoning restrictions and existing structures that might inhibit their construction. Additionally, residential and commercial operations that might be impacted by their operation must also be addressed in some respect as well. Hence, attempting to build and deploy FSS applications in developed markets can be problematic but building and deploying them in developing markets is much simpler.

d. While revolutionary at their introduction, overseas containers have become a necessary and vital part of the shipping process but are also now inefficient by many standards. Overseas containers may arrive to developed markets full of product but they must be sent back to these high-volume producing nations empty by the same vessels that deliver them. They must also be transported back to ports by truck and rail empty so that they can be returned to these high-need markets.

e. FSS may be a physical transportation solution but it is a physical application that is automated through its IT infrastructure and platform. This is the primary characteristic within FSS solutions that facilitate autonomous operation in the first place. A technical operator that already works within a logistics firm has only to integrate the system monitoring of the FSS into his or her daily routine rather than putting into place an entirely new logistics team.

f. All for-profit enterprises are under a mandate to remain both profitable and growth minded for investors. Solutions that enable for-profit firms to do so can and should be embraced wholeheartedly by a firm's executive leadership. In terms of international benchmarks, logistics solutions like the FSS allow for-profit enterprises to accomplish these types of financial performance mandates.

g. The Kingdom will benefit significantly from more progressive social policies. Likewise, quality of life factors have the potential to stimulate the current workforce to produce more, expend less and become more accountable to the commercial enterprises that employ them. Combined these factors are meant to foster an environment that engenders creativity, innovation and productivity within the Kingdom.

h. The value chain is an important strategic element in managing logistics. The value chain allows logistics operators to identify what activities are important to manage and which ones can be set aside or minimized.

i. RFID is a very old technology that has been renewed by the development of newer technological applications and platforms. RFID falls into the realm of near-field communications which may be dominated today by newer platforms such as Bluetooth but RFID existed both in practice and concept prior to the age of computers and the microchip.

j. It is often the case that shrink (a concept that refers to the reduction in available supply within a supply chain) occurs not necessarily to damage or theft but often just simple loss. In many instances supply chains are so long, complex and multifaceted that product can simply be misplaced. RFID applications, as long as they are functional, prevent loss and misplacement of product within the supply chain.

k. RFID technology use in the retail sector has really opened up an enormous number of possibilities as well. Retailers found that RFID chips could be placed in shopping carts as a means to signal various stations scattered throughout a store to light up and show ads and coupons when consumers pushed by with their carts for instance.

l. China is not the only market that has become synonymous with counterfeit goods but it has begun to separate itself from other countries with poor records by eliminating many counterfeit producing firms. Initially such producers flourished after China's acceptance into the WTO which led to many firms relocating their manufacturing and production there in order to leverage China's comparative advantage in labor. Therefore, regardless of the risk of counterfeit goods, many firms the world over benefited economically from China's low wage costs and the long-term effect of such competitive production economics.

m. The automation of the supply chain is of course the Holy Grail of any logistics provider and supply chain operator. However, absolute automation is not yet possible in most instances and actual workers are still very much a part of the process of the transportation and shipment of products and as such they often go places in the supply chain where technology infrastructure is not.

Industry Resources

7 Unexpected and Awesome Uses of RFID Tags. **RFID Arena**. http://rfidarena.com/2014/3/4/7-unexpected-and-awesome-uses-of-rfid-tags.aspx

An Overview of the EPCGlobal Network. **IEEE**. http://ieeexplore.ieee.org/document/6601749/?reload=true

Analysis: RFID Technology in Logistics & Supply Chain. **Arabian Supply Chain**. http://www.arabiansupplychain.com/article-12080-anlysis-rfid-technology-in-logistics-supply-chain/

Applications of RFID Technology in the Logistics & Supply Chain Industry. **Barcoding Incorporated**. https://www.barcoding.com /blog/the-applications-of-rfid-technology-in-the-logistics-supply-chain-industry/

Bagloee, Saeed Asadi, et al. "Autonomous vehicles: challenges, opportunities, and future implications for transportation policies." *Journal of Modern Transportation* 24.4 (2016): 284-303.

Benefits and Drawbacks in Using the RFID (Radio Frequency Identification) System in Supply Chain Management. **Modelling, Computation and Optimization in Information Systems and Management Sciences**. https://link.springer.com/ chapter/10.1007/978-3-319-18167-7_16

Dekker, Rommert, et al., eds. *Reverse logistics: quantitative models for closed-loop supply chains*. Springer Science & Business Media, 2013.

DuoSkin. **MIT**. http://duoskin.media.mit.edu/

EPCGlobal. **GS1**. https://www.gs1.org/epcglobal

Fernie, John, and Leigh Sparks. *Logistics and retail management: emerging issues and new challenges in the retail supply chain*. Kogan page publishers, 2014.

Frequently Asked Questions. **RFID Journal.** http://www.rfidjournal.com/site/faqs

Gordon, Michael S., et al. "Controlling driving modes of self-driving vehicles." U.S. Patent No. 9,566,986. 14 Feb. 2017.

Govindan, Kannan, Hamed Soleimani, and Devika Kannan. "Reverse logistics and closed-loop supply chain: A comprehensive review to explore the future." *European Journal of Operational Research* 240.3 (2015): 603-626.

How RFID Tags Became Trendy. **Engadget.** https://www.engadget.com/2017/08/22/rfid-tags-in-fashion/

"Is Logistics the Same as Supply Chain Management?" Michigan State University: Eli Broad College of Business Management (2017). Retrieved from: https://www.michiganstateuniversityonline.com/resources/supply-chain/is-logistics-the-same-as-supply-chain-management/#.WeioyWi3yUk

Logistics News. **RFID Journal.** http://www.rfidjournal.com/logistics

The Many Amazing Uses of RFID Technology. **ITProPortal.** http://www.itproportal.com/2016/06/23/the-many-amazing-uses-of-rfid-technology/

Mangan, John, and Chandra Lalwani. *Global logistics and supply chain management.* John Wiley & Sons, 2016.

Radio Frequency Identification (RFID) Technology. **Technologies of Control.** https://www.le.ac.uk/oerresources/criminology/ msc/unit8/page_20.htm

Research on Supply Chain Management Based on RFID Technology. **Management Science and Industrial Engineering International Conference.** http://ieeexplore.ieee.org/document/5707569/

Rushton, Alan, Phil Croucher, and Peter Baker. *The handbook of logistics and distribution management: Understanding the supply chain.* Kogan Page Publishers, 2014.

Saudi Vision 2030. **Arab News.** http://www.arabnews.com/category/tags/saudi-vision-2030

Saudi Vision 2030. **Kingdom of Saudi Arabia.** http://vision2030.gov.sa/en

Stadtler, Hartmut. "Supply chain management: An overview." *Supply chain management and advanced planning.* Springer Berlin Heidelberg, 2015. 3-28.

"Supply Chain Management Essentials (SCME)." CSCMP: Council of Supply Chain Management Professionals (2017). Retrieved from: http://cscmp.org/CSCMP/Educate/CSCMP/ Educate/Online_ Courses.aspx?hkey=1df75e7e-12a8-400d-9f56-2feb7ac0fb42

Urmson, Christopher Paul, Michael Steven Montemerlo, and Jiajun Zhu. "Detecting road weather conditions." U.S. Patent No. 9,110,196. 18 Aug. 2015.

What is RFID? **EPC-RFID Info.** http://www.epc-rfid.info/rfid

What's in Saudi Arabia's Blueprint for Life After Oil? **Bloomberg.** https://www.bloomberg.com/news/articles/2016-04-25/key-elements-of-saudi-arabia-s-blueprint-for-life-post-oil

Whitmore, Andrew, Anurag Agarwal, and Li Da Xu. "The Internet of Things—A survey of topics and trends." *Information Systems Frontiers* 17.2 (2015): 261-274.

Yan, Rui, and Rui Yan. "Optimization approach for increasing revenue of perishable product supply chain with the Internet of Things." *Industrial Management & Data Systems* 117.4 (2017): 729-741.

Endnotes

1   Saudi Vision 2030. 2017. Saudi Government. Retrieved from: http://vision2030. gov.sa/en/node/60

2   Are Drones the Future of Marine Surveying? Martek-Marine (online). Retrieved from: https://www.martek-marine.com/blog/are-drones-the-future-of-marine-surveying/

3   Montreuil, B. (2017). Omnichannel Business-to-Consumer Logistics and Supply Chains: Towards Hyperconnected Networks and Facilities. *Progress in Material Handling Research.*

4   Amazon PrimeAir. 2017. Amazon.com (online). Retrieved from: https://www. amazon.com/Amazon-Prime-Air/b?node=8037720011

5   González-Jorge, H., Martínez-Sánchez, J., & Bueno, M. (2017). Unmanned Aerial Systems for Civil Applications: A Review. *Drones, 1*(1), 2.

6   Chopra, S. & Meindl, P. (2016). Supply Chain Management: Strategy, Planning and Operation. Pearson, New York.

7   Ranger, S. (2016). This is How Google Drones Will Deliver Your Packages and Keep Your Pets Safe. ZDNet, 01(27), pp.18-24.

8   Kaufman, L. (2017). Ports Go Electric in Drive to Decarbonize and Cut Pollution. *Inside Climate News*, 07(17), pp.07-10.

9   Kavli, Per, and Mike Welch. "A Novel Solution to Deepwater Logistical Challenges: Fast Supply Shuttles and High Bollard Pull AHTS." *OTC Brasil.* Offshore Technology Conference, 2013.

10 Saudi Fund in Initiative for Better Use of Robots. (2017). *Arab News*, 09(07), pp.17-21.

11 The Freight Shuttle System: A 21st Century Solution to Freight Transportation Challenges. *Texas A&M Transportation Institute*. Retrieved from: https://tti.tamu. edu/freight-shuttle/

12 Kavli, Per, and Mike Welch. "A Novel Solution to Deepwater Logistical Challenges: Fast Supply Shuttles and High Bollard Pull AHTS." *OTC Brasil.* Offshore Technology Conference, 2013.

13 The Solution. (2017). Freight Movement Redefined: Clean, Safe, Smart. *Freight Shuttle.* https://www.freightshuttle.com/the-fss-solution/the-solution/

14 Rezaei, Niloofar. *COMPARISON OF CONSTRUCTION METHODS FOR BUILDING AN UNDERGROUND FREIGHT TRANSPORTATION IN TEXAS.* Diss. 2016.

15 Nair, P. R., & Anbuudayasankar, S. P. (2016). Tackling Supply Chain Management Through RFID: Opportunities and Challenges. In *Proceedings of the International Congress on Information and Communication Technology*(pp. 467-475). Springer Singapore.

16 Gleghorn, G. D., & Harper, A. (2015). Logistics and Supply Chain Management and the Impact of Information Systems and Information Technology. In *Technology, Innovation, and Enterprise Transformation* (pp. 295-301). IGI Global.

17 Shin, S., & Eksioglu, B. (2014). Effects of RFID technology on efficiency and profitability in retail supply chains. *Journal of Applied Business Research, 30*(3), 633.

18 Ozdemir, A., & Bayrak, M. A. (2015). Assessment of RFID Investment in the Military Logistics Systems Through The Life Cycle Cost (LCC) Model. *Journal of Military and Information Science, 3*(4), 88-102.

19 Muslimah, M. D., & Simatupang, T. M. (2014). Supply chain collaboration for ensuring retail product availability at Glaxosmithkline. In *6th International Conference on Operations and Supply Chain Management.*

20 Shin, S., & Eksioglu, B. (2015). An empirical study of RFID productivity in the US retail supply chain. *International Journal of Production Economics, 163,* 89-96.

21 Govindan, K., Soleimani, H., & Kannan, D. (2015). Reverse logistics and closed-loop supply chain: A comprehensive review to explore the future. *European Journal of Operational Research, 240*(3), 603-626.

22 Della Cava, Marco. "$1.7 Trillion in Fake Goods: That's Alibaba's Uphill Battle." *USA Today,* 01/16(2017): pp.07-09.

23 Fox, Brooke. "How Kodak-Backed Startup eApeiron is Fighting Fakes With Invisible Ink." *The Economic Times,* 09/29(2016): pp.08-09.

24 Fox, Brooke. "How Kodak-Backed Startup eApeiron is Fighting Fakes With Invisible Ink." *The Economic Times,* 09/29(2016): pp.08-09.

25 Xiao, Eva. "Blockchain Meets Fashion in Bid to Fight the Fakes." *TechinAsia* (online): 2017. Retrieved from: https://www.techinasia.com/bitse-vechai n-blockchain-anti-counterfeiting

26 Kinninmont, Jane. "Vision 2030 and Saudi Arabia's Social Contract: Austerity and Transformation." *Middle East and North Africa Programme,* 07/01(2017): p.11.

27 Yan, Rui, and Rui Yan. "Optimization approach for increasing revenue of perishable product supply chain with the Internet of Things." *Industrial Management & Data Systems* 117.4 (2017): 729-741.

28 Li, Bo, and Yulong Li. "INTERNET OF THINGS DRIVES SUPPLY CHAIN INNOVATION: A RESEARCH FRAMEWORK." *International Journal of Organizational Innovation (Online)* 9.3 (2017): 71B.

29 Skilton, Mark. *Building digital ecosystem architectures: a guide to enterprise architecting digital technologies in the digital enterprise.* Springer, 2016.

30 "Smart Glasses New Standard in Order Picking." *Supply Chain* 24-7, 08/04(2017): pp.07-12. Retrieved from: http://www.supplychain247.com/article/smart_glasses_new_standard_in_order_picking/Wearable_Technology

31 Jones, Richard. "2018: The Year of Wearable Technology in the Supply Chain." *Supply & Demand Chain Executive*, 01/25(2016): pp.18-24.

32 Bruno, T. (2015). *Wearable technology: Smart watches to Google Glass for libraries* (Vol. 1). Rowman & Littlefield.

33 Kao, H., Holz, C., Roseway, A., Calvo, A. & Schmandt, C. (2016). DuoSkin: Rapidly Prototyping On-Skin User Interfaces Using Skin-Friendly Materials. *ACM*, 09/12-16, pp.1-8.

34 Drahl, Carmen. "The Surprisingly Simple Chemistry in DuoSkin, Temporary Tattoos That Control Your Phone." *Forbes*, 08/16(2016): pp.17-21.

35 Gresham, Tom. "The Who, What, When, and Why of Warehouse Wearables." *Inbound Logistics*, 01/17(2017): pp.04-07.

36 "Economic Cities: Opening Vistas of Growth in the Kingdom of Saudi Arabia." *EY—MENA*, 07/01(2015): pp.1-26.

37 Tavana, Madjid, et al. "Drone shipping versus truck delivery in a cross-docking system with multiple fleets and products." *Expert Systems with Applications* 72 (2017): 93-107.

38 "E-Commerce." *Saudi Post* (online). Retrieved from: https://sp.com.sa/en/E-Commerce/Pages/EMall.aspx

39 Berman, Jeff. "FedEx, USPS Extend Air Transport Contract to 2024." *Supply Chain* 247, 02/24(2017): pp.17-17.

40 "Mission & Vision." *EMS* (online). Retrieved from: http://ems.com.sa/en/about/mission-and-vision

41 Palma-Mendoza, Jaime A., Kevin Neailey, and Rajat Roy. "Business process re-design methodology to support supply chain integration." *International Journal of Information Management* 34.2 (2014): 167-176.

42 Pal, Brojeswar, Shib Sankar Sana, and Kripasindhu Chaudhuri. "Three stage trade credit policy in a three-layer supply chain–a production-inventory model." *International Journal of Systems Science* 45.9 (2014): 1844-1868.

43 Dewar, Robert D., et al. "UPS Supply chain solutions." *Kellogg School of Management Cases* (2017): 1-19.

44 Dewar, Robert D., et al. "UPS Supply chain solutions." *Kellogg School of Management Cases* (2017): 1-19.

45 Hozak, K. (2012). Managerial guidance for applying RFID in the tourism industry. *Interdisciplinary Journal of Contemporary Research in Business*, 4(2), 18-30.

46 "USPS Seeking Suppliers to Provide Info, Solutions on New Sensor Technology for Mail Tracking." *Postal Reporter* (online). Retrieved from: http://www.

postal-reporter.com/blog/usps-seeking-suppliers-to-provide-info-solutions-on-new-sensor-technology-for-mail-tracking/

47 Ferrer, G., Dew, N., & Apte, U. (2010). When is RFID right for your service?. *International Journal of Production Economics, 124*(2), 414-425.

48 Ramesh, B., Utpal Baul, and V. Srinivasan. "An approach to bolster up the logistic link of supply chain in cement industries through value engineering techniques." *Indian Concrete Journal*(2016): 79.

49 Ming, C. (2006). The enterprise value analysis based on reverse logistics. *SEI Online*, 330013.

50 Eckstein, Dominik, et al. "The performance impact of supply chain agility and supply chain adaptability: the moderating effect of product complexity." *International Journal of Production Research*53.10 (2015): 3028-3046.

51 Siham, Lakri, et al. "Designing supply chain performance measurement and management systems: A systemic perspective." *Advanced Logistics and Transport (ICALT), 2015 4th International Conference on.* IEEE, 2015.

52 Johnson, S. (2007). Implementing the environmental value engineering process in the built environment. *University of Florida*, Department of Engineering.

53 Berman, Jeff. "Walmart's New On-Time Delivery Standards May Create Supply Chain Challenges for Its Suppliers." *Logistics Management,* 09/07(2016): pp.11-14.

54 "Business Services." *EMS* (online). Retrieved from: http://ems.com.sa/en/business-solutions/business-services

55 Hozak, K. (2012). Managerial guidance for applying RFID in the tourism industry. *Interdisciplinary Journal of Contemporary Research in Business, 4*(2), 18-30.

56 Siham, Lakri, et al. "Designing supply chain performance measurement and management systems: A systemic perspective." *Advanced Logistics and Transport (ICALT), 2015 4th International Conference on.* IEEE, 2015.

57 Siham, Lakri, et al. "Designing supply chain performance measurement and management systems: A systemic perspective." *Advanced Logistics and Transport (ICALT), 2015 4th International Conference on.* IEEE, 2015.

58 "GS1 Standards in Transport and Logistics." *GS1 AISBL,* 07/01(2017): pp.1-24.

59 Yin, R. K. (2011). *Applications of case study research.* Sage.

60 Greiner, Martin. *Automotive Supply Chain Management in the Internet of Things.* GRIN Verlag, 2015.

61 "Internet of Things in Logistics." *DHL Trend Research/Cisco Consulting Services,* 07/01(2015), pp.1-29.

62 Lee, In, and Kyoochun Lee. "The Internet of Things (IoT): Applications, investments, and challenges for enterprises." *Business Horizons* 58.4 (2015): 431-440.

63 Gubbi, Jayavardhana, et al. "Internet of Things (IoT): A vision, architectural elements, and future directions." *Future generation computer systems* 29.7 (2013): 1645-1660.

64 Gubbi, Jayavardhana, et al. "Internet of Things (IoT): A vision, architectural elements, and future directions." *Future generation computer systems* 29.7 (2013): 1645-1660.

65 "Internet of Things in Logistics." *DHL Trend Research/Cisco Consulting Services,* 07/01(2015), pp.1-29.

66 "Jubail Industrial City." Bechtel Corporation (online). Retrieved from: http://www.bechtel.com/projects/jubail-industrial-city/

67 LaValle, Steve, Eric Lesser, Rebecca Shockley, Michael S. Hopkins, and Nina Kruschwitz. "The IOT, analytics and the path from insights to value." *MIT Sloan Management Review* 21 (2013).

68 Russom, Philip. "The IOT analytics." *TDWI Best Practices Report, Fourth Quarter* (2011).

69 Kavis, Mike. "The Internet of Things Will Radically Change Your The IOT Strategy." *Forbes,* 06/26(2014): pp.8-11.

70 Minelli, Michael, Michele Chambers, and Ambiga Dhiraj. *The IOT, big analytics: emerging logistics intelligence and analytic trends for today's logisticses.* John Wiley & Sons, 2012.

71 Morby, Alice. "Saudi Arabia Becomes First Country to Grant Citizenship to a Robot." CNBC News (online). Retrieved from: https://www.dezeen.com/2017/10/26/saudi-arabia-first-country-grant-citizenship-robot-sophia-technology-artificial-intelligence-ai/

72 Chen, Shang-Liang, Yun-Yao Chen, and Chiang Hsu. "A new approach to integrate internet-of-things and software-as-a-service model for logistic systems: A case study." *Sensors*14.4 (2014): 6144-6164.

73 Banker, Steve. "Robots in the Warehouse: It's Not Just Amazon." *Forbes Magazine,* 01/11(2016): pp.18-22.

74 MacCarthy, Bart L., et al. "Supply chain evolution–theory, concepts and science." *International Journal of Operations & Production Management* 36.12 (2016): 1696-1718.

75 Stamp, Jimmy. "Robotics and Fulfillment Centers Are Reshaping Retail—and Cities Could be Next." *The Architect's Newspaper,* 08/23(2017): pp.07-11.

76 Montreuil, Benoit. "Omnichannel Business-to-Consumer Logistics and Supply Chains: Towards Hyperconnected Networks and Facilities." *Progress in Material Handling Research* (2017).

77 Qiu, Hang, et al. "Augmented Vehicular Reality: Enabling Extended Vision for Future Vehicles." *Proceedings of the 18th International Workshop on Mobile Computing Systems and Applications.* ACM, 2017.

78 Roberts, Jack. "First Look: Tesla's All-Electric Semi Truck." *HDT: Heavy Duty Trucking,* 11/16(2017): pp.18-21.

79 Green, Jemma, and Peter Newman. "Citizen utilities: The emerging power paradigm." *Energy Policy* 105 (2017): 283-293.

80 Govindan, Kannan, Hamed Soleimani, and Devika Kannan. "Reverse logistics and closed-loop supply chain: A comprehensive review to explore the future." *European Journal of Operational Research* 240.3 (2015): 603-626.

81 Martin, James, et al. "Certification for autonomous vehicles." *Automative Cyber-physical Systems course paper, University of North Carolina, Chapel Hill, NC, USA* (2015).

82 Wietfeld, Christian, et al. "Smart Grids." *IEEE Wireless Communications* 24.2 (2017): 8-9.

83 Kim, Baekgyu, Shinichi Shiraishi, and Jonathan Shum. "Dynamic Virtual Objective Generation for Testing Autonomous Vehicles in Simulated Driving Scenarios." U.S. Patent No. 20,170,286,570. 5 Oct. 2017.

84 "Level Diagram." SAE (online). Retrieved from: http://www.sae.org/misc/pdfs/automated_driving.pdf

85 Bedinger, Melissa, et al. "Human Factors in the Supply Chain." *Logistics Research Network Conference,* 09/3-5, pp.1-9.

86 Brandon-Jones, Emma, et al. "A contingent resource-based perspective of supply chain resilience and robustness." *Journal of Supply Chain Management* 50.3 (2014): 55-73.